GAY MEN AT WORK

A report on discrimination against gay men in employment in London

by Phil Greasley

Contributions from:
Matt Williams
S Kumar
Terry Munyard
Winston Hunte

Cartoons by Dave Robinson
Cover design by Rif

ISBN 0 9511149 1 3

Typeset by Lasso Women's Co-operative (TU), 86-100 St Pancras Way, NW1 01-267 1284
Printed by Trojan Press workers' co-operative (TU), 25 Downham Rd, London N1
01-249 5771

■ Contents

■ Foreword

For years we have instinctively known that gay men face intense discrimination in employment. In recent months this has intensified yet further, as gay men face the onward march of the AIDS virus and the added discrimination and prejudice — born largely out of ignorance — that has come with it. We have known this in our hearts; but we haven't had the clearly documented facts to back up what our commonsense and the evidence of our eyes and ears told us.

This survey now gives us those documented facts. And the results are chilling; they should give us all pause for thought. 78 per cent of those surveyed said they did not state that they were gay when they last applied for a job, revealing the fear, the anxiety, the self-protective shell, that gay men and lesbians are so often forced to adopt in a hostile world. Six per cent of the survey had been sacked *for being gay*. And the redress open to them through supposed equality legislation and industrial tribunals turned out all too often to be negligible.

Quite apart from the bare statistics, the personal accounts and interviews movingly tell us more about the experiences, the moods, the frustrations, the hostilities; they add a lot to the drier data produced by the survey, and help to paint a fuller — if grimmer — picture.

This survey comes at an important time. It will help to make clear the argument about why the law has to be strengthened to prevent discrimination on grounds of being lesbian or gay: it demonstrates convincingly that protection against such forms of discrimination is much weaker than against others. It gives us the facts with which to back up our arguments about the way discrimination operates. It charts clearly how much worse things have become with the onset of the AIDS crisis. It gives us all a sense of what it is like to be sacked or abused or shouted at or laughed at or treated with contempt.

It will also, I hope, give all who read it a renewed sense of determination to overcome the prejudice and the hostility and the injustice. That will be its greatest service, and it accordingly gives me the greatest pleasure to welcome the survey and commend it to you.

Chris Smith MP
August 1986

■ Acknowledgements

We would like to thank all the organisations and individuals who have given help, support and advice for the report. Special thanks to — the Greater London Council and the London Boroughs Grants Scheme for funding LAGER and this report, to our support group, past and present, for giving up their own free time, to Microsyster for help with computing, to Lesbian Employment Rights (LER), the Gay London Police Monitoring Group (GALOP), the Terrence Higgins Trust (THT) and the Campaign for Homosexual Equality (CHE) for advice, to Lasso for typesetting this report and being very patient. Many thanks to every gay man who took the time to fill in the questionnaire and all the gay men interviewed — without you there would be no report.

Space does not allow us to mention every individual who helped us with the report but we would especially like to thank: Trevor for proof reading and endless other bits and pieces, Roya, Nina and Anne for lots of practical help and guidance, Brian for his part in initiating the research and early work on it, Will for help with interviewing, Brendan for making time to help whenever needed and Tony for his patience with Matt.

■ Introduction

Lesbian and Gay Employment Rights (LAGER) is a project fighting the discrimination faced by lesbians and gay men in employment and unemployment. LAGER has been funded by the London Boroughs Grants Committee since April 1986 and prior to this was funded by the Greater London Council. There are separate lesbian and gay sections in LAGER. Lesbian Employment Rights (LER) is an autonomous section of LAGER which deals with issues specifically related to discrimination faced by lesbians in un/employment. All lesbians are discriminated against by heterosexism and sexism. It is the experience of sexism which distinguishes the discrimination faced by lesbians from that experienced by gay men. Therefore, the autonomy of LER is vital.

The work of both sides of LAGER involves:
- Giving advice, help and information to individuals who have problems or queries related to employment. Where appropriate, individuals are referred to sympathetic legal advisers or other relevant bodies.
- Liaison with trade unions, local authorities and voluntary organisations. Much of this work has centred around the promotion, discussion and drafting of equal opportunities policies and their implementation.
- Campaigning work to counter heterosexism generally in the field of employment.
- Research into various aspects of un/employment.

LER RESEARCH
LER has already published a report on anti-lesbian discrimination in un/employment in London called "All In A Day's Work". The LER report is based on a survey and follow-up interviews with lesbians. It is an account of the range of discrimination faced daily by many lesbians — anti-lesbianism, racism, sexism, and discrimination on the grounds of disability, class and status as mothers.

GAY MEN AT WORK
This report is based on research carried out by the gay men in LAGER into the experiences of gay men in un/employment in London. The report looks at some of the many ways in which gay men face discrimination in employment and makes recommendations for how this discrimination can be overcome. It must be strongly emphasised that an understanding of anti-lesbian discrimination cannot be gained from reports which relate experiences of, and issues relevant to gay men. Because of this, we recommend that "Gay Men at Work" is read in conjunction with the LER report.

Throughout the report and in all the work of LAGER we try to stress that the fight against anti-gay discrimination should be one part of the struggle

We have tried to balance the lack of depth inherent in this type of question-naire by conducting taped interviews with gay men on a one-to-one basis (*See section on Interviews, below*).

Distribution of the questionnaire
2,000 copies of the questionnaire were distributed. Two main methods of distribution were used. First we sent batches of the questionnaire to a variety of lesbian and gay organisations in London for them to distribute for us. Second we handed out copies of the questionnaire to gay men who attended certain lesbian and gay events, for example Gay Pride Day, June 1985.

The lesbian and gay organisations who received batches of the questionnaire for distribution included 13 lesbian and gay trade union groups, 15 lesbian and gay voluntary organisations and 2 gay orientated shops. The groups and organisations distributed the questionnaires in a variety of ways. Some groups simply distributed the questionnaires to their members, whereas the London Lesbian and Gay Centre and the two gay shops were able to have piles of questionnaires for clientele and customers to pick up when visiting these places. The questionnaires were distributed over the summer of 1985. The closing date for completed questionnaires was October 31st, 1985.

The method of distribution means that the sample is not a random sample. There is not enough known about the demographic features of gay men to achieve a random sample. The method for distributing the questionnaire also means that it cannot be representative of all the gay communities in London, (*See Personal Characteristics, page 3*).

Survey response
By October 31st, 1985 we had 200 completed questionnaires for analysis. Two questionnaires had been rejected, one because the respondent did not define himself as gay, the other because the respondent worked in Amsterdam and had filled in the questionnaire while on holiday.

The places and organisations where respondents obtained their ques-tionnaires are shown in Table 1. (Page 3)

Interviews
Face-to-face interviews were conducted to give a wider and more detailed impression of the experiences gay men have at work. We asked respondents to the questionnaire to indicate if they would be willing to be interviewed further by LAGER. Owing to a lack of time it was not possible to interview every gay man who said he would be willing. 17 gay men who responded to the questionnaire were interviewed face-to-face.

As can be seen below in the section on personal characteristics, the majority of respondents to the questionnaire were white. In an attempt to address issues relevant to Black gay men, LAGER approached some Afro-Caribbean Black gay men to be interviewed. The responses to these interviews have only been partially included into the report. However, LAGER intends to redress this imbalance in its future work.

All the face-to-face interviews were conducted by using a list of

2

open-ended questions which covered the same subject areas as the survey questionnaire. We assured the interviewees of confidentiality, if required, and conducted these interviews with only the interviewer and interviewee present. All of the interviews with Black gay men were conducted by a Black gay man. Each interview was recorded on tape and transcribed at a later date. At all times the interviewee was encouraged to direct the interview as he wanted to, and not to feel limited by answering only the questions asked. The interviews lasted between 30 and 90 minutes. The length obviously depended on how much the interviewee had to say about his experiences. Some interviewees related experiences about more than one job.

TABLE 1

Organisation	No. of Respondents
London Lesbian and Gay Centre	39
Gay's The Word Bookshop	46
Body Tec (gay retail shop)	25
Gay Pride Day, June '85	28
GLC Jobs For A Change Festival	5
Greenwich Lesbian and Gay Day	6
Lambeth Lesbian and Gay Town Hall Disco	3
London Friend and Switchboard	4
Other Voluntary Organisations + TU Groups*	24
Questionnaires distributed via LAGER (Workers and Management Council)	20
TOTAL REPLIES USED	200

* Other/Voluntary/TU groups are CPSA Lesbian and Gay group; London Gay Teenage Group; Gay Men's Disabled Group; Gay Teachers Group; Teachers in Further Education Gay Group; NCCL Gay Rights Committee.

PERSONAL CHARACTERISTICS
This section looks at the characteristics of gay men who answered the questionnaire. It has been divided into three different areas:
1. Race, disability, class and age;
2. Employment status, employers and occupations;
3. Moving to, and living in London.

Race, disability, class and age
Race
Nearly 9 out of 10 gay men in the survey are white, non-Irish gentiles. Of the 198 gay men answering this question, only 4 indicated that they are Black gay men, 4 that they are Jewish and 18 that they are Irish. 4 respondents indicated that they are "a member of another ethnic group". 99 per cent said their first language was English.

Gay men with disabilities
7 per cent of the gay men in the survey defined themselves as "a person with disabilities". Thus more than 9 out of 10 respondents did not define themselves as such.

AGE

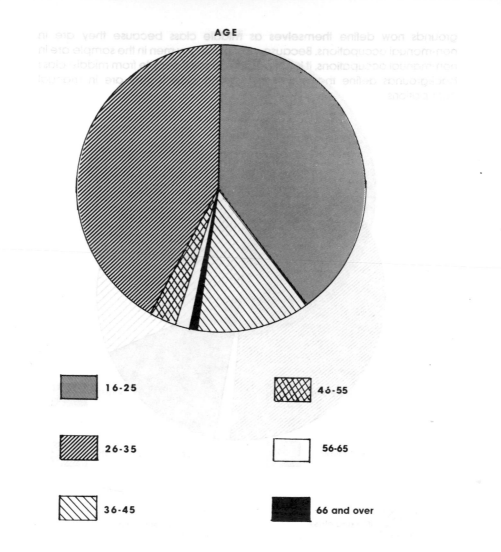

▨ 16-25		▨ 46-55	
▨ 26-35		☐ 56-65	
▨ 36-45		■ 66 and over	

Summary and remarks
Briefly the results are that:

- Nearly 9 out of 10 respondents are white, non-Irish gentiles;
- More than 9 out of 10 respondents define themselves as people without disabilities;
- Half of the gay men in the survey define themselves as middle class;
- 40 per cent of the gay men in the sample were under the age of 26.

The sample of gay men in the survey vastly over-represents the views and experiences of white, middle class, non-Irish gentiles, who define themselves as without disabilities. The survey therefore is not representative of gay men who suffer discrimination as a result of more than one type of oppression.

Why the biases?

Much of the bias in the representation of views and experiences in the survey is because of the design and distribution of the questionnaire. The questionnaire was designed by white, non-Irish gentiles without disabilities. All of the questions about the attitudes and experiences are asked only in relation to being gay men. Gay men who also suffer from discrimination because of their race and/or disability and/or class may see questions which relate only to their experience of being gay at work as irrelevant or inappropriate to them. A questionnaire which asks for gay related incidents only, ignores the cumulative effect of multiple oppression. Equally, the discrimination experienced because of heterosexism may seem less important to some gay men than other forms of discrimination they face.

Many of the places where the questionnaires were distributed are places frequented by a high proportion of gay men who are actively involved, to some extent, in lesbian and gay politics. The political movement is still dominated by white, middle class, non-Irish gentiles, without disabilities. Although we believe this situation is now changing, such change happens all too slowly.

The age distribution of the sample is, in terms of the male population, biased towards younger gay men. This is not a bad thing — the views of young people are often ignored. It should be stated, however, that since the advent of the "gay liberation" movement in the late 'sixties, it has been relatively easier to lead a gay life style than in previous years. The age distribution in the survey reflects this trend towards the greater participation of younger gay men in the lesbian and gay political movements.

Employment status, employers and occupations

20 of the respondents were unemployed at the time of filling in the questionnaire (10 per cent). 6 of the unemployed gay men in the survey stated that they had never been employed since leaving school or further education. 9 of the 20 unemployed answered the questionnaire as if they were still employed in the last job they had been in.

One respondent was retired but answered questions relating them to his last job. Two of the respondents were students. 177 of the gay men were employed at the time of the survey. Two of these were self-employed.

Employers

Over half (51 per cent) of the gay men who named their employer worked for public sector employers. In Table 2 (a breakdown of the employers of the gay men in the survey) the public sector employers are divided into three broad categories.
1. Local Authorities etc. This group comprises Councils, Local Health Authorities, Local Education Authorities and Institutes of Higher Education.
2. Government Departments and DHSS.
3. Other Public Services. In this survey only London Underground and London Regional Transport were mentioned in this category.

The "Other" category in Table 2 comprises two self-employed, two co-operative workers and one trade union worker.

TABLE 2
Employers of the gay men in the survey

Employers	Number of gay men	Percent (%)
Private Employers	53	41
Voluntary Sector	6	5
Local Authorities etc.	50	38
Government Departments	14	11
Other Public Sector	3	2
Other	5	4

The Table includes 9 unemployed respondents and 1 retired respondent who answered the questionnaire as if they were still in their last job. 56 respondents did not state who their employer was. Those answering the questionnaire as unemployed or as students are excluded from the Table.

Occupations

We did not ask for detailed information about occupations. Of those gay men who stated their occupation (159 respondents) the majority were in non-manual work (92 per cent, including shop work). Of those in non-manual work the highest proportion were in clerical work (30 per cent).

Summary and remarks

- 10 per cent of the gay men in the survey were unemployed;
- More than half of the respondents who named their employer were working for the public sector;
- More than 9 out of 10 respondents who stated their occupation were in non-manual jobs. Clerical work was the most frequently stated occupation.

The number of unemployed respondents must not be taken to indicate the rate of unemployment amongst gay men. The questionnaire is geared to employed gay men and would more than likely seem irrelevant to unemployed people. Respondents who tried to fill in the questionnaire from the point of view of being unemployed were often forced to leave large sections of the questionnaire blank.

The high proportion of gay men in the sample who are in non-manual work reflects the middle class bias in the sample to some extent. It should also be taken into account that over 50 per cent of the employed population in London are now in non-manual jobs. It should not be assumed that non-manual jobs have better pay or conditions than manual jobs.

Moving to and living in London

19 per cent of the gay men in the survey had lived in London all their lives. 7 per cent of the sample worked in London but lived outside the area. The remaining 74 per cent had moved to London from other areas. Of those moving to London, 4 out of 5 had moved to London in the last 10 years. Two-thirds of the gay men who had moved to London said that being gay was an important reason for moving here.

Household

Half of the gay men in the sample said they lived with lesbians and/or other gay flatmates. This figure includes gay men who live with their lovers. Nearly a quarter of the gay men in the sample live alone. Most of the remainder lived with heterosexual flatmates, relatives, or a combination of the above categories.

Summary and remarks

- Nearly three-quarters of the gay men in the sample had moved to London from other areas;
- Two-thirds of the gay men who had moved to London said that being gay was an important reason for doing so;
- Half of the gay men in the sample lived with lesbian and gay flatmates only. A further quarter lived alone.

There are many reasons why being gay is an important reason for moving to London. One is moving to be with other lesbians and gay men. There are large lesbian and gay communities in London and there are relatively more amenities for us than in smaller towns and cities. For gay men there are more pubs, clubs, discos and shops. There are also relatively more non-commercial, non-profit making venues and groups.

Another important reason why gay men move to London relates to its being a huge, diverse and cosmopolitan city. Because of these features it has a reputation for being generally more "liberal" than smaller towns and cities. Such a reputation may lead gay men to believe that they will suffer less harassment in London for being gay, a belief which may relate as much to expectations of gaining employment and being accepted in it, as it does to their leisure time.

■ Chapter Two
Gay workers and the law

This chapter looks at the legal position of gay men in relation to employment. The law is discussed from two angles, first by looking at our lack of rights and lack of protection in employment law; second, by looking at the way gay men can have their employment or employment chances affected by laws which openly discriminate against us.

EMPLOYMENT LAW

A lack of protection
In theory all workers have the right not to be unfairly dismissed by their employers. But for lesbians and gay men who are sacked on account of their sexuality this right is of little practical use. It is very difficult to mount a legal challenge to any employer who sacks, demotes, refuses to employ, or discriminates against people simply on the grounds that they are lesbian or gay. Decisions to dismiss lesbians and gay men have usually been upheld by industrial tribunals, especially in cases where employees have contact with children in the course of their work.

The Employment Protection (Consolidation) Act 1978 requires employers to prove that an employee has been dismissed for a reason which the law regards as fair. Reasons which the law considers acceptable are —

- A reason related to the employee's capability (that is, skill, aptitude, health, physical or mental qualities, for example) or qualification for the job;
- A reason related to the employee's conduct;
- That the employee is redundant;
- That the employer could not continue to keep the worker in the post she or he holds without contravening a particular statutory duty or restriction, e.g. the requirement to have a driving licence in order to work as a driver;
- That there is "some other substantial reason" which would justify dismissal.

Given such a wide range of possible reasons for dismissal, it is not difficult for an employer to find grounds for sacking any employee. Employers who wish to dismiss lesbians and gay men may claim that the dismissal is, in fact, on account of conduct or capability, rather than sexuality, or they may argue that the fact that someone is lesbian or gay is sufficient for the "some other substantial reason" category.

Having shown that they have a potentially fair reason for dismissal, employers must pass a further legal test — the "reasonableness" test. Section 57 of the Employment Protection (Consolidation) Act 1978 says —

I spent three years in the Royal Navy. I was arrested and put on detention for being gay, tried and dismissed from service. (Radiographer)

I did not get promotion, along with other out gays, until a homophobic head of division was removed. Promotion quickly followed for me along with other gays. (Local government housing officer)

I was charged with gross indecency. Two months before my trial the possibility of my promotion arose. The principal of my college told me I could not be promoted "with this hanging over me". When I was acquitted I was promoted but he then denied that my trial had ever been a factor which they considered. (College lecturer)

I was moved and demoted upon failing positive vetting for being open about being gay. (Civil servant)

I was put on disciplinary procedures for unsatisfactory performance, but it turned out to be victimisation and was resolved in my favour with the help of my union, BIFU. (Bank clerk)

There is no way of knowing just how many men are sacked, demoted, or refused promotion on the grounds that they are gay. Publications and reports which attempt to catalogue cases of discrimination can only draw upon incidents which have been reported in some way. Most incidents go unreported. In addition, there are many cases where being gay has not been given as a reason for dismissal, but has been a major factor influencing the employer's decision. Such incidents can be very difficult for employees to prove or sometimes even to realise.[2]

ARMED FORCES

All sexual contact between members of the same sex is illegal for members of the armed forces. Sexual contact is illegal whether the person is on or off duty, or on leave. It is irrelevant to the law whether the other party or parties involved are members of the forces or civilians. In the merchant navy sexual contact is illegal between crew members of merchant ships but not between a crew member and a passenger.[3]

Many gay men join the forces at an age when they are not fully aware of their sexual preferences. Some who are aware may not realise the consequences of being gay in the forces. Once in the forces, being suspected of being, or being discovered to be gay can lead to gross maltreatment and humiliation.[4]

In 1984 there were at least 87 administrative discharges for "homosexual conduct" in the armed forces (this figure is for both women and men). There were at least six dismissals or dismissals with disgrace for homosexual conduct (all men), both of which can be damaging for future job prospects. Employers are often suspicious when documents read "services no longer required".

The arguments used by the Ministry of Defence to retain the ban on lesbians and gays are that a) it prevents the coercion of junior personnel into homosexual practices by senior members of the forces; b) homosexual practices have a disruptive influence.

Neither of these arguments holds any weight. There are sufficient regulations already in existence in the armed forces to deal with "disruptive" or coercive practices regardless of whether or not the situation involves sexuality.

It is *not* the intention of this report to press for changes in the law in order to encourage gay men to join the forces. We *do* believe, however, that all gay men should have the right to practise their sexuality on a parity with heterosexuals and this includes those who are in the armed forces.

SEXUAL OFFENCES

Gay men are often arrested and charged with criminal offences which have no heterosexual equivalent. Publicity accompanying such charges and/or the possession of a criminal record can cause difficulties for gay men at work and looking for work.

The discriminatory nature of the criminal law against gay men has been well documented in other recent literature.[5] Therefore this subject is dealt with only briefly here.

Sex between two consenting men, over the age of 21 and in private, was decriminalised in England and Wales in 1967 by the Sexual Offences Act. Subsequent legislation for Scotland followed in 1981 and for Northern Ireland in 1982. On this legislation Paul Crane comments:

> In general terms, the law conceded that if two "adult" men wanted to go to bed in their own homes then that alone should not be a crime any more. These measures did not reflect an acceptance of homosexuality, rather the extent and method of control was refined.[6]

In respect of gay men, the criminal law now focuses on sexual behaviour in "public" places and on relationships between "adults" (over 21) and young men (under 21).[7]

The commonest criminal laws used against gay men are the offences of importuning and gross indecency. The police also use the Public Order Act to prevent displays of affection between gay men in public on the grounds that this is insulting and will lead to a breach of the peace. They rely, too, on loosely-worded by-laws prohibiting "indecency", and on offences of inciting or procuring acts of gross indecency — i.e. asking someone if he wants to have sex.

It must be strongly emphasised that these are all, or almost all, consensual offences, sometimes called victimless crimes. There is no element of forcing someone into any kind of behaviour against his will, and the vast majority of these cases involve either two men willingly having sex together, or one man inviting another, usually in fairly discreet terms, to go to bed with him. These "offences" are often detected only by means of elaborate police observation from inside public lavatory broom cupboards or by means of plain clothes officers putting themselves among gay men with a view to

In our survey of gay men and employment we asked the following question — "If you were charged with an offence which has no heterosexual equivalent, e.g. for having sex with someone over the age of 16 but under the age of 21 do you think your employer would use this against you?"

76 respondents said they thought their employer would use such offences against them (46 per cent of those who answered the question). The next question asked respondents if they thought their union would support them in such an instance. 70 respondents did not think their union would support them (44 per cent of those who answered the question).

40 respondents (20 per cent of the sample) said that their employers included lesbians and gays or sexual orientation in their job advertisements or literature. Of these people only 11 thought that their employers would use such an offence against them (30 per cent).

Working with children

The stigma attached to the possession of a criminal record for a "sexual offence" can be particularly harmful for gay men who work with, or who are applying for jobs to work with children. Organisations whose work involves children often have access to information about the police records of potential employees. Statutory bodies, for example, local authorities and education authorities, can draw upon three sources of information to check if there are reasons why someone should not be employed to work with children. These are:

a. Direct contact with the police for information about criminal convictions;
b. "List 99". This is a list, drawn up by the Department of Education and Science, of people who may not be employed as teachers or as any other workers in the field of education. The information is not based solely on criminal convictions and includes substantiated allegations of misconduct;
c. DHSS consultancy service. This is an advisory service which holds a register of people deemed unsuitable for employment in the child care field. The information on the DHSS register comes from police records, reports by local authorities and voluntary organisations, and the "list 99" described above.[10]

The system of disclosure of criminal convictions of those with access to children is currently under review. The review was begun in early 1985 by the Home Office and the DHSS. A first report by the Home Office and the DHSS, published in July 1985,[11] recommends that checks on the background of people working or volunteering with statutory organisations should be carried out with local police forces. A steering group has now been set up, which includes members of voluntary organisations, to discuss how this system might be extended to, and used in, voluntary organisations. At the time of going to press the steering group is still at the discussion stage.

It is clearly important for any organisations whose work involves contact with children to be provided with a means of checking the suitability of potential or existing employees. The problems which arise from the disclosure of criminal records to employers or to consultative bodies lie in the interpretation of such records. For example, in a society which stereotypes gay men as "child molestors", it is likely that records which disclose sexual offences of *any* kind will be assumed to show an unsuitability for work with children. In the light of our earlier discussion about the consensual nature of the vast majority of "sexual offences" between gay men, it is essential that a system of checking is devised which objectively differentiates between relevant and irrelevant offences.

SUMMARY AND RECOMMENDATIONS

Employment law

Under present employment law lesbians and gay men can be sacked, demoted or refused promotion simply because they are lesbian or gay. We believe the law needs to be changed to make discrimination against lesbians and gay men illegal. However, it is absolutely crucial that a change in law designed to protect lesbians and gay men in employment mentions lesbians and gay men specifically as the groups to be protected and does not specify protection on the grounds of "sexual orientation". The importance of not using "sexual orientation" is clear if we consider the Sex Discrimination Act (1975) and the Race Relations Act (1976). On many occasions these Acts have been used against the groups they were designed to protect. For example, the Courts have in the past allowed claims from men that they have been discriminated against under the Sex Discrimination Act because employers have recruited women, especially where issues of positive discrimination were involved.

Industrial tribunals

In the interests of all employees, legislation which relates to unfair dismissal needs to be reviewed.

The term "unfair dismissal" is itself a misleading term. What is judged is not the fairness or unfairness on the sacked worker but simply whether the employer has applied standards of a "reasonable employer" in deciding whether to dismiss — regardless of how unfair it may be on the particular worker. The tribunal cannot find the dismissal unfair, even if all three of its members would not have dismissed in the same circumstances, provided the employer has acted within the "range of reasonable responses" available to any reasonable employer. In other words the industrial tribunal cannot put itself in the employer's shoes and judge the case, all it can do is ask — was dismissal in these circumstances something no reasonable employer would have done? Such procedures give an unfair bias to employers and need to be reviewed and changed.

Many other rules and regulations involved in cases of dismissal give an unfair bias to employers. For example, many employees are unable to fight their dismissal at tribunals because they have not worked for their employer long enough to qualify for a hearing. Cases of dismissal brought on the grounds of race or sex discrimination or trade union membership or certain other specified exceptions do not require a qualifying period. Any attempt to change the law to make unlawful the dismissal of lesbians and gay men on the grounds of sexuality must ensure that there is no minimum qualifying period of continuous employment before a complaint can be brought against an employer.

19

Composition of industrial tribunals

Many lesbians and gay men are deterred from taking cases of dismissal to industrial tribunals because they think they have no chance of winning. An examination of past cases involving the dismissal of lesbians and gay men reveals that industrial tribunal panels have, on several occasions, accepted reasons from employers which are blatantly heterosexist as "reasonable" grounds for dismissal. Whilst a law making it illegal to dismiss on the grounds of being lesbian or gay would help to change this situation, such a law would need to be backed up by a change in the statutory requirements for the composition of tribunal panels.

The current statutory requirement for a tribunal panel hearing a case is that it should comprise a legally qualified chairperson and two lay members. One of the lay members must be drawn from representatives of employers and the other from representatives of employees. These are the only statutory requirements and there is no obligation for tribunal panels to reflect employers or employees in terms of their race, sex, class, being lesbian or gay, or people with disabilities.[12]

The statutory requirements for the composition of industrial tribunals would need to be changed if the law were amended to make it unfair to dismiss on the grounds of being lesbian or gay. At the very least there should be a requirement that the lay members of the tribunal representing employees' interests should attempt to reflect the applicant bringing the case in terms of race, sex, class, disability and/or being lesbian or gay. To achieve such aims there would obviously have to be a pool of lay members available to sit on tribunals who represent a spread of all the discriminated groups in the community. This would have to be taken into account in future appointments to tribunal panels.

Appointments to tribunals

Lay members are appointed to industrial tribunal panels every three years by the Secretary of State for Employment and are nominated by sponsoring bodies. The sponsoring bodies which nominate lay members for the employees' side are the Trades Union Congress (TUC) and The Managerial, Professional and Staff Liaison Group (MPG).

The current three-year appointments come to an end in October 1986 and some new appointments will be made. An Employment Gazette article records that in March 1986 there were approximately 2,150 lay members on industrial tribunal panels of whom only 400 were women and 25 were from ethnic minorities. In view of the forthcoming new appointments, the article states that:

> Ministers are encouraging the sponsoring bodies to put forward more suitably qualified candidates who are women and people from ethnic minorities.[13]

There is no reason why trade unions should feel obliged to wait for a change in the law before they act to ensure that lesbians and gay men and other oppressed groups are represented on tribunal panels. The TUC and the MPG should extend the Department of Employment recommendation quoted above to include lesbians and gay men and people with disabilities.

To be effective, the sponsoring bodies must develop a policy, worked out with relevant groups in the community, which seeks to ensure that the lay members nominated redress the existing imbalance on tribunal panels.

Sexual offences

Criminal law discriminates against gay men, and can have consequences for gay men in employment or looking for work.

The police have exploited these laws to gain arrests of gay men. Judging by their practice to date, the police are unlikely to change their tactics unless the law itself is changed. The discriminatory laws can affect gay men at work if their employers get to know about the alleged "offence". The LAGER survey shows that many gay men *do* fear that their employers would use such offences against them.

Many of the laws which discriminate against gay men are to be found in the Sexual Offences Acts of 1956 and 1967.

These Acts need to be totally revised and changed to give equal status to gay men under the law. Particular aspects of the Act which need to be repealed are, for example, the sections which deal with gross indecency and importuning (Sexual Offences Act 1956 ss 13 and 32). The laws relating to the age of consent and privacy should be brought into line with equivalent heterosexual laws. Overall, the law should not deem unlawful any sexual contact between members of the same sex which is lawful between members of the opposite sex. The repeals and revisions should also apply to members of the Armed Forces.

Working with children

The system of disclosure of criminal convictions of those with or wishing to have access to children is currently under review. (The review was set up by the DHSS and the Home Office and is described earlier). One of the main purposes of the review is to extend the right of disclosure to all organisations whose work involves children (thus both statutory and voluntary bodies).

It is essential that all organisations whose work involves access to children have a system of checking the suitability of employees or potential employees. The dangers of disclosure are, however, that convictions irrelevant to working with children may be considered to show an unsuitability for employment. The police have made it clear that in providing information to organisations they cannot take on the responsibility to decide which convictions are relevant to working with children.[14] Thus, once information was requested, the police would provide the entire criminal record regardless of its content. It is important that a system of disclosure is devised which does not allow the personal prejudice of employers or consultative bodies to influence the decision to employ. A system could include, for example, statutory guidelines to be introduced to ensure safeguards against discrimination and to introduce an element of standardisation.

There needs to be an assurance that only "correct" or "accurate" information is provided and that employees or job applicants can know what is disclosed and challenge it if it is wrong. Any dismissal based on incorrect information should be automatically unfair. In the past there have been examples of the police selecting names wrongly or confusing the records of people with the same name.

Employers

It is important generally that employers and organisations have an understanding of the way criminal law is used to discriminate against gay men. Employers must be aware that the vast majority of "sexual offences" between gay men are consensual and have no victims.

Employers and organisations who are developing Equal Opportunities Policies (explained in chapter 5) should ensure that the recruitment and promotion procedures ignore such "offences".

Chapter Three
Day-to-day work

The last chapter concentrated on the dismissal and demotion of gay men as a consequence of laws which discriminate against us. This chapter is about the day-to-day situations that gay men find themselves confronted with at work. The situations described are quotes from the interviews with gay men and quotes from written responses to the survey questionnaire. The gay men interviewed were asked various questions about the attitudes of people they worked with or worked for. Most of the gay men quoted in this chapter work in non-manual occupations. Many of the jobs talked about by the interviewees are in sectors of industry which employ a majority of women. Attempts were made to interview gay men who work in areas of employment which are dominated by men. These attempts were, however, largely unsuccessful.[1] There is a need for more research in this area.

COMING OUT AT WORK

From the replies it would seem that most gay men do not state they are gay when applying for jobs. 78 per cent (151) of the gay men who answered the questionnaire said that the last time they applied for a job they did not state they were gay.

The results of the questionnaire show that being openly gay at work is important for gay men. 90 per cent of the respondents said they would like to be openly gay at work (many of them already were). 78 per cent said they would like to be openly gay when interviewed for jobs. It is important to remember, however, that most of the responses to this question were given by white gay men. The responses in the face-to-face interviews with Black gay men indicated that they may be reluctant, or opposed to coming out at work because they see racism as a priority issue. The work with Afro-Caribbean gay men identified many false assumptions made about gay men. The Black gay men interviewed were keen to point out that not all gay men are white. As Winston pointed out,

"I do feel that Black gay men are ignored. They're ignored by both Black and white communities and that includes white gay communities. Many white people still have notions about Black people's sexuality which have continued since the days of slavery. Black men are often seen as having a 'strong, mysterious and exotic sexuality'. Some white gay men still see Black gay men in this light. Despite this idea of 'exotic' sexuality all the other racist assumptions about Black gay men are there as well — ideas that we can't be trusted and are only out for money or whatever.

In Black communities homosexuality is often thought to be a 'white western disease' despite the fact that homosexuality exists as much in Caribbean and African societies as anywhere else — even if it is less overt. The Black person coming out therefore finds lack of support in their own community as it is perceived that this is deflecting from the main issue of fighting racism within the white community."

Coming out as gay at work would not need to be an issue if it were not for two major assumptions made by society generally. First, it assumes that anybody who is not heterosexual belongs to a group which is somehow inferior. For many gay men, coming out at work involves weighing up the pros and cons of being openly gay with workmates and with employers. The decision to come out at work is often dependent on the type of work environment gay men are in. If there are hostile and anti-gay attitudes prevalent in the workplace, the process of coming out can be a very difficult one. Coming out can be at the risk of being ostracised by other workers or even dismissed by employers. Some gay men may decide against coming out at work because of the trouble it could cause them. Gay men who experience forms of discrimination alongside heterosexism, may have different perceptions about the notion of coming out. For example Jim, a Black gay man, saw the issue of coming out quite differently from Michael and Gary, two white gay men.

Jim (unemployed)
"Being Black and gay doesn't affect me because I don't come out... Future chances of employment (are) affected by my being Black but not being gay."

Michael (Punch operator DHSS)
"When it's come down to it I've not applied for jobs because I knew the employer's feelings. I couldn't go for a job in industry, for instance, because I have to be open about being gay and I knew I wouldn't get it because of that. So any job that discriminates I can't go into, because I have to be out. I can't be closeted."

Gary (Trade Union Support Group Worker)
"If I'm looking for a job I'd want one where I wouldn't be likely to have any hassle for being gay. I don't think I could be closeted at work. I'd resent to have to be, as well."

24

There are different degrees of being openly gay at work. Whereas some gay men are open with everyone they work with, including their employers, many others may choose to be openly gay with only a few of the people they work with, people with whom they may have developed a friendship or trusting relationship. Some of the gay men interviewed talked about the decision to come out at work or not to.

Terry is a charge nurse. He tells his experience of coming out in a hospital.
"When I used to be a staff nurse I was fairly openly gay. That is, I used to talk about being gay to colleagues who were on the same grade as me. When I was promoted to a charge nurse I felt in a more secure position, especially to challenge prejudice. I hate falsehood, so whereas the others would talk about their boyfriends and girlfriends, I would talk about my lover in the same way. Every time I got new people there I didn't make a point of going to them and saying 'I'm gay', but, during conversations I'd just mention my lover.

When people realise I'm gay, they are often quiet because they don't really know what to say. If they are male they often go red! If they are new to the area and just talking generally about, for example, buying a house in the area and their wife still lives in so and so, then I have said things like 'Oh yes, my lover and I would like to have a house there'. That sometimes stops the conversation dead! Some of the people are all right, some are very straightforward."

Kevin is a residential social worker who left Ireland about three years ago to live in London. He comments about the difference between coming out in London and in Ireland.
"In my present job they employed me knowing I was gay. My gayness came up in the interview. I think that it is a very good example of the level that we're at. With the people I work with I think it is clear that I am gay. For me, there is nothing to hide as such. It is not an issue in that I don't rush up to people and say, 'Hi, my name's Kevin and I'm gay'. That's unimportant, but most people, presumably, will realise.

I've had no problem with the people I work with. I've had no slashed comments or scathing remarks. It's quite an open subject. We have a laugh more than anything else. There's quite a lot of banter and that's quite funny. Gay things are talked about in a sort of tongue-in-cheek, funny sense. Like someone will say, 'Oh well, we all know what he wants, don't we'. It's in a funny sense which is good although it can often sidelight what people's real feelings are.

Ireland was a completely different kettle of fish. In Ireland it was impossible to work in residential work and to be openly gay because the channels are not there to be open about it. The degree of openness I have in London, I could never have in Ireland, particularly in residential work. A lot of that stems from ignorance of the difference between paedophilia and homosexuality. I think that doubt exists to some extent in London, and even perhaps with the people I'm working with. I think perhaps at the back of people's minds there is a doubt. I think there is a need for educating people."

Ken is a librarian who found that it was relatively easy for him to be openly gay at work because there was an openly gay man already on the staff.

"Because I've worked there a long time I've now sort of established myself and I'm openly gay with everybody. Before I worked there I knew somebody there already and they were openly gay so to an extent they'd done a lot of the ground work; the staff there were fully aware of gay rights, gay issues, and they were aware of having a gay man in their midst. I arrived and he left shortly afterwards and I just sort of took over. But I am openly gay with everybody."

Bill is a clerk and general administrative assistant. He talked about a decision made not to be openly gay in one of his previous jobs as a clerk.

"I've never been one for saying 'take note I am gay' but if someone has asked me I've said yes. At one place, however, I didn't say I was gay for a variety of reasons. They looked as gays as being perverse, a load of 'pouftahs' and didn't want anything to do with them. Every six weeks or so it used to be brought up. I thought, well sod it I'll have nothing to do with it. I was actually asked one or two times if I was gay and I just said, 'I'm not answering that question'. But then the graffiti appeared in the lift, 'Bill is gay', and things like that. I just ignored it. Although I'd like to be one of those people who's quite radical and would like to change people's attitudes in the workplace and so on, it would not have worked there. It's very difficult when you're one of 80 people in the workforce to take on the whole bloody lot!"

John is a chief technician in a university. He has made the decision not to be openly gay with most of the people he works with because of the generally hostile atmosphere.

"Coming out at work could be a bit awkward. I wouldn't mind if the staff weren't so antagonistic generally, general backbiting and so forth. There is a gay couple who work in another section. It's known that they co-habit etc, and it's a general subject of ridicule behind their backs and occasionally to their face. I can see the result or guess if it were me in that situation."

HETEROSEXISM AT WORK

This section represents some examples of the heterosexism that gay men have to face in their day-to-day work situations. The examples are from the in-depth interviews given by gay men. There are obviously endless ways in which heterosexism expresses itself and these accounts should in no way be taken to represent all the ways in which gay men are discriminated against at work.

Lack of understanding
Michael (Punch operator)

"When I told the people at work that I was gay, most of them were okay to start with — well, all of them. With some, however, I've found out that it's just a front. The most common thing I've come across is a lack of understanding and a lack of knowing what's going on. Most of them think we don't get any prejudice because we are gay. They nearly dropped dead when I told them some of the things that had happened to gay friends of mine."

Heterosexism and lack of support

In the LAGER survey of gay men in employment, 23 per cent said that none of the people they worked with were particularly supportive of their being gay. A further 46 per cent said only some were supportive. Only seven per cent said that all of the people they worked with were particularly supportive while 24 per cent said that most were.

When gay men do find themselves faced with heterosexist and homophobic attitudes they are often left to fight their own battles. Terry and Ainsley illustrate the point.

Terry

"I've had one or two problems with people's attitudes. I've had support from people when I've been on my own, but they wouldn't support me openly. For instance, as part of my work, we look at the social situation of patients. Before the consultant's round which deals with the medical problems, we look and see if any of the patients have got social problems.

This is a group that involves physiotherapists, therapists, usually the consultant, junior doctors, hospital social worker and a nurse input as well. During one of these meetings the consultant was not present. A junior doctor at the meeting is in some ways 'aggressively heterosexual'; he is very much a 'Cor! Look at her!' sort of person. He referred to a patient saying, 'Such and such a patient is queer'.

He knew that I was gay, he is supposed to be educated, and he needn't have even mentioned that about the patient. It wasn't relevant to the situation at all. I felt the remark was made to knock me in some sort of way, or made as a challenge. I said, 'Hold on, the use of that terminology is derogatory and I'm not happy with that at all. The proper neutral terminology is gay'. This was in a room full of people. His response was to turn to me and say, 'I don't care what you think'. There was absolute silence in the room. I didn't know quite what to do. The comment really shut me up.

I was so angry I couldn't carry on work after the meeting. Later the social worker who had been quite friendly to me, and had always gone on about the fact that her next door neighbours were a gay couple and they were good friends etc, she said, 'I was really upset when he said

The doctor, social workers, therapists and nurses meet to discuss their patients... and at the same time show support for a colleague!

that'. I said, 'Well, you or anyone else didn't stand up for me'. She was silent. Various people could see what had happened. Even in asking what had happened the response was quite odd. One enrolled nurse I work with asked what had happened. I told here what the doctor had said. Her response was, 'Just because he was single why should he say that he was queer', missing the point entirely!"

Ainsley (telephonist)

"I was working in a clothes shop as a sales assistant. One day one of the other assistants was serving a woman who asked if her little boy could go to the toilet. There was only the staff toilet at the back of the shop, but when you're working on commission you'd do anything for a sale, so I took the little boy to it so that the other assistant could carry on serving the woman.

The child was three or four years old so he didn't need me to help him, so I just put him in and shut the door. The toilet was next to the staff room, so I went into the staff room and stood talking to the people there. About ten to 15 minutes later he hadn't come out, so I went in to see if he was all right and then went back into the staff room. About five minutes after that the women came downstairs just as the child was coming out of the toilet. Apparently he'd just been sitting there 'cos there was no toilet paper.

When the woman went I said, 'She was a bit dramatic, wasn't she?'. The assistant said that the women asked, 'Is my child safe with him down there?' and he said to her 'Yes, he's okay, I think he prefers them a bit older than that!'. Everyone in the staff room laughed except for two Black women who were good friends of mine. I said, 'I am glad you find it so funny to be accused of being a child molester'. I was really pissed off because all these people were supposed to be my friends.

I thought it really brings it home to you how few heterosexuals there are who are prepared to stand up for you in a crowd. Incidents like that make me far more aware of my gayness. It seems to make cliches like 'How dare you presume I am heterosexual' really make sense, 'cause you know you've got to really fight for yourself when it comes to the crunch 'cause no one else will fight for you."

Nothing but sex

It seems to be commonly believed that gay men are constantly looking for sex 24 hours a day. As a result gay men find themselves suspected of having, or trying to procure all sorts of sexual liaisons, even at work. The suspicions and assumptions can affect the respect given to gay men by co-workers and employers.

Ken (librarian)

"I used to work with another gay man and we had a lot of personality clashes simply on professional matters. After he'd left we found that everybody assumed the reason we didn't get on was because we'd had some sort of sexual liaison that had gone disastrously wrong and therefore all this flack was just sexual nastiness. It wasn't so much the people I work with but people in the system as a whole. A very subtle form of oppression that people assume that two gay men who don't get on have got something going on between them that's gone wrong."

Tom (now a student)
"I was a housing worker for a short life housing co-op in Earls Court. The co-op was run by a collective and everyone in the collective was straight apart from me. Whilst there I faced a certain amount of harassment, insinuation and discrimination from all the 'straight' collective. This was because of my attempts to get them to house more of the homeless gay young people in that area. At the time of my appointment in May '81 only 14 per cent of the licensees housed by the co-op were gay — that figure was always under threat because of the 'problem of housing young gays'. I had several allegations made against me by my fellow workers — one of them that I was attempting to create a 'male brothel' by housing known 'rents' (male prostitutes). Several times I was threatened with dismissal for attempting to make the housing co-op's policy more representative in such a heavily gay area."

Terry
"I'm in the position as a charge nurse where I supervise many students. As part of this work I have to give a report at the end of their period on the ward. There was an incident where a male student nurse, who has a reputation for his amorous heterosexual activities throughout the hospital, did not maintain a very high standard in his work or attitude. I had had to warn him during his period on the ward that I didn't think that his work was up to scratch and to try and improve things. He knew that I would have to give him a bad report. I wrote the report and called him into the office to talk about it. So he said to me, 'If I offer to sleep with you, would you write a better report?'. I said, 'No, to get a good report you have got to be a good nurse, that's the way it is'. I thought about the situation and what I should do about it. I knew that I would be quite within my rights to go to the school of nursing and speak to my line manager and say, 'This is an instance where someone is trying to use the fact that I am gay to their advantage'. I thought seriously about it, but came to the conclusion that if I did take it further it could only damage me. It was a situation where there was nobody else present and nobody overheard it. The student could have turned round and said that I had told him that I would give him a better report if he slept with him. Because he had such a reputation as a heterosexual and I have a reputation as a homosexual, therefore I think the tendency would have been to believe him."

Dealing with the public
There are many jobs which involve dealing with the public. Gay men often face insults and abuse from customers, clients and patients they work with.

Terry

"There was one patient who had acute bronchitis and needed oxygen all the time. Despite this, he kept creeping out of the ward for a cigarette. I told him he was being a fool because after every cigarette he had to spend the next three hours on oxygen! He said, 'And what are you? You're just a pansy.' So although I'm out with colleagues, because of the relationship I have with patients, I can't take up their prejudices."

Ainsley

"Because I work in social services I don't get many problems from the people I work with. However, I work on reception and I do get abuse from the public. Like today, for instance, I had this really bad experience from this one woman, she was really nasty. She called me 'a fuckin' queer' and '… all queers are child molesters…'. She was just going on like she was mad. That doesn't happen a lot, but it *does* happen. The two women who work immediately with me were really supportive. One of them screamed, 'I'd much rather trust him with my children than with someone like you'."

Heterosexual men and machismo

Many of the gay men interviewed talked about the bigoted views of heterosexual men — views which seem to go hand in hand with keeping up a 'macho' image. Any man who does not conform to the rules of machismo is treated with contempt or ridicule.

Bill (Admin worker)

"I used to work for British Gas. There was an equal opportunities group set up by a workers' collective and they wanted changes on the job application form. For example, they said it wasn't necessary to know whether or not a person was single, married or divorced. They produced a statement asking for changes, which I thought was very good, which got circulated around all the members — it was a closed shop.

One of the engineers said to me, 'What interest is that to the working man, gays, Blacks and lesbians? They want to fill the place with a load of black dykes'. He wasn't the type of bloke you go up to and say, 'Well, what's wrong with Black lesbians?'. He was only interested in the 'working man' and the macho image that goes with it and everything else.

Then there was another bloke usually not very forceful in his views. He was vehemently opposed to it and I said, 'What's wrong with it?' He said, 'Well, if I was employing people I'd want to know if they were married, single or blah, blah, blah'. I said, 'Why?' He said, 'I want to know what they are'. And I said, 'What do you mean, what they are?', and he said 'Well, whether they're gay or straight…' (he used the word gay and I was quite surprised) 'because some people might have strong objections to working with them'. I said, 'Well, if you were an employer don't you think it might be nice to get other people to look at it and say, well there's nothing wrong with people being gay, it's just a sexual preference and people here are going to learn there's nothing wrong with it'. He said, 'No, no, no, people have got ideas against it and it's all right being in a minority but keep it in the family'.

Generally speaking, the women there were far more interested in change than the men. However the department was very heavily dominated by men."

Ainsley

"When I came out I was working at Telecom. Once I decided I was gay, or found out why I was different from other people, a lot of people stopped talking to me, and didn't want to know me. Suddenly people stopped inviting me to their houses. In Telecom there are a lot of gays and they're fine — gays are acceptable to work with and they're a laugh but not to have them in your house and socialise with, you know, it's touchy ground.... It's not so much women but their husbands and boyfriends."

Steven

"When I was a credit controller — I still had girlfriends then, which was a bit ironic — the manager used to be sly and unpleasant in sneaky ways at my expense. Because he was a bit odd it seemed to give the other staff licence to be a bit hostile. When new employees started the manager would say, 'This is Stephanie' and I'd say, 'No it's not, it's Steven. Don't say that!' He'd then take exception saying I criticised him! There was a beauty competition of girls' clothes once and he said, 'I expect you're going to enter it, aren't you!' and things like that which seemed a bit strange for someone of his responsibility."

Fucking queers, poufs, pansies and child molesters. All familiar terms of abuse. Abuse, insults and ridicule are deliberate and obvious ways of showing homophobia and heterosexism.

More subtle, often not deliberate, heterosexism is more difficult for straight people to realise within themselves. The subtle forms of discrimination are often based on assumptions made about gay men, and on a lack of understanding. All major institutions — the family, the education system, and the church — teach heterosexuality as the only acceptable way of life. Lesbians and gay men are largely ignored or portrayed in a negative way. Heterosexuality as the only acceptable norm is reinforced by the media, which constantly put out false and misleading information about lesbians and gay men based on misinformation and myths.

Challenging heterosexism involves individuals taking responsibility for challenging their own attitudes and behaviour. From an organisational point of view much can be done to challenge heterosexism by the introduction of an Equal Opportunities Policy designed to fight discrimination on the grounds of being lesbian or gay. Equal Opportunities Policies are equally important for employers and trade unions. The chapter on Equal Opportunities (Chapter 5) details the type of measures employers can take to fight discrimination. Similarly, the chapter on trade unions (Chapter 6) recommends ways in which trade unions can take on board issues of heterosexism.

Chapter Four
AIDS

In the past two years no excuse has been used more to discriminate against gay men than AIDS and the myths surrounding this disease.

This chapter concentrates on the problems gay men have faced in jobs because of AIDS hysteria. Work should be seen in context, however, as only one of the many areas where gay men have suffered discrimination because of AIDS hysteria. Gay men have been refused and evicted from housing and accommodation because of fear of AIDS. On the streets gay men have been subject to an increase in physical and verbal attacks. Shouts of "AIDS scum" and "AIDS-ridden bastard" have become commonplace to people leaving lesbian and gay pubs. The fear of contracting AIDS has even been used as an excuse by a heterosexual man for the murder of a gay man.

In many cases AIDS has been used as an excuse to express prejudice which already existed against lesbians and gay men. Notwithstanding this, there has developed a fear of AIDS or "AIDS phobia" amongst many people in Britain. The fear of AIDS has been generated by one major source, the media. No opportunity has been missed by the popular press to use "Hammer Horror" tactics to scare people about AIDS. Front page headlines have reported AIDS as a "gay plague" or a gay disease.

AIDS is not a "gay plague" or a gay disease. It is becoming a major public health problem in this country which affects everyone. It is everybody's responsibility to help fight the disease and halt it spreading. Before people can take responsibility they need to have the facts about the disease, especially, how it can be spread.

The first part of this chapter gives some general information about AIDS. The second part looks at the type of reactions gay men have faced at work since the advent of AIDS.

PART I
WHAT IS AIDS?[1]

AIDS (Acquired Immune Deficiency Syndrome) is a rare condition which seriously damages, at present irreversibly, the body's immune system. Owing to the damage incurred by the immune system, the body becomes unable to fight a number of serious diseases, for example, certain types of cancers. The syndrome is considered to be caused by a virus called HIV (human immuno deficiency virus). The virus has previously been called HTLV III or LAV.[2]

The antibody test

There is no test available to the public which can say whether or not you have the HIV virus. The only test available is one which tests for antibodies to the virus in the blood. Antibodies are the human body's own response to the virus. Research has shown that most people who have HIV antibodies in their blood do have the virus in their body. The only conclusion, however, that can be definitely drawn from a positive result to the test is that the person has been exposed to the virus at some time or another.

Tests to date indicate that the majority of people who have the virus remain well. It is estimated that only one in ten of the people who have a positive result to the HIV antibody test go on to develop AIDS. A slightly higher proportion (about 15 per cent) will develop either:

a) The fairly minor illness, Persistent Generalised Lymphadenopathy (PGL). The main feature of PGL is that the lymph glands in the neck and armpit remain swollen for a minimum of three months; or

b) AIDS related complex (ARC). This complex covers a variety of illnesses which fall short of the definition of AIDS.

The rest of the people who show positive to the HIV antibody test remain perfectly well and healthy (about 75 per cent).

Passing the virus
Evidence currently suggests that the HIV virus is only transmitted from person to person via blood or semen.[3] Only four methods of transmission have been proven:
- Sexual contact, between the same and the opposite sex;
- The injection or transfusion of blood or blood products taken from infected persons (usually factor VIII, which is the blood product for clotting absent in haemophiliacs);
- Sharing injection needles with an infected person;
- Transfer of the virus from mother to baby. Babies born to infected mothers are often also infected and have a high probability of developing AIDS.

Who is at risk?
Certain groups of people have suffered disproportionately from HIV infection and from AIDS in comparison with the wider population. Again it must be reiterated that within each of these groups the numbers of people with AIDS is small in comparison with the total numbers in each group.

In America and Europe the groups most at risk are gay and bisexual men, haemophiliacs, intravenous drug users who share needles, recipients of blood transfusions, and babies born to antibody positive parents.

AIDS is found in several African countries (especially Uganda and Zaire). In Africa AIDS seems to be spread mainly by heterosexual contact. Thus anyone who has had heterosexual sex in central Africa in the last few years, while visiting or living there, is part of another risk group.

Low risk
The group at a lower risk than any other section of the population is lesbians. Despite being at a lower risk, lesbians have also suffered discrimination as a consequence of the AIDS hysteria. The fact that AIDS is being used to discriminate against lesbians is clear evidence that the nature of AIDS discrimination is firmly based in heterosexism and homophobia. The discrimination due to AIDS and AIDS hysteria is not related only to the fear of disease. AIDS is being used, particularly by the media, to legitimise prejudice against lesbians and gay men.

AIDS and the work environment

The ordinary, non-sexual, person to person contact that occurs in everyday work situations poses no risk to workers, customers or clients for the transmission of HIV virus.

The HIV virus does not survive well outside of the body. The virus must get right into the blood stream for infection to take place. The virus is not airborne, or infectious by casual contact. AIDS cannot be contracted by, for example:

- Shaking hands, sharing drinking and eating utensils, or by sharing washing and toilet facilities;
- Coughs and sneezes do not pass on the virus.

It may seem common sense that a disease which is still very rare in the population cannot be passed on by the above methods. If AIDS *could* be passed on so easily it would now be as widespread as the common cold. The interviews quoted later, however, show that such myths of transmission have become popular beliefs encouraged by the hysteria of the popular press.

Food service workers

Food service workers have often been assumed to be at a greater risk of HIV infection than other workers. There is no evidence to back up this belief. For health and safety reasons good standards of hygiene should obviously be maintained. However, if standards of hygiene are not maintained workers and customers become in danger of catching many other diseases more easily transmitted than the HIV virus.

Health care workers

People whose work includes contact with patients, their blood or other bodily fluids should take precautions broadly similar to those followed by people taking care of hepatitis B patients. The Royal College of Nursing has prepared guidelines for those caring for people with AIDS.[4]

There is no reason why anybody should be sacked because they are antibody positive. First, people who are positive do not put other workers at risk of infection. Second, most people who are antibody positive remain well and therefore able to work as usual. If an antibody positive employee does become unwell standard entitlements to sick pay and leave should apply.

PART II
GAY MEN AND PUBLIC REACTIONS TO AIDS

Reactions gay men have had at work because of AIDS hysteria range from snide comments and jokes to actually being sacked. This section begins with the results of the questions about AIDS hysteria in the LAGER survey of gay men and employment. It then goes on to record just some of the comments and situations that gay men have faced at work due to AIDS phobia. The accounts and comments are from the interviews with gay men and from comments written on the gay men's questionnaire. It is by no means an exhaustive account of all the situations, comments and sackings that have occurred.

The survey

41 of the respondents to the gay men's questionnaire said that the public reaction to AIDS had changed the circumstances in which they work. 48 gay men said that the public reaction to AIDS had changed their inclination to come out as gay at work.

Coming out

In the chapter on day-to-day work we looked at the decision whether to come out at work or not. For many gay men who are not already out at work, the AIDS hysteria has made the decision to come out even more difficult.

"I still feel strongly that it is important to come out, but I feel obliged to be fully informed about AIDS before coming out with certain less than sympathetic people." (College lecturer)

"Hostile reactions to gays because of AIDS makes it more difficult to come out at work. At the same time there is real pressure to give blood donations. I have been challenged as to why I don't and I may have to tell them." (Civil servant)

"I am now working as a youth worker which makes it difficult to be 'out' about being gay, but much more difficult now because of AIDS." (Youth worker)

"From the way the AIDS 'jokes' have proliferated and anti-gay feeling has increased it could be a tactical error to come out at work!" (Theatrical house manager)

"I feel because of AIDS and the Fleet Street reaction to it, I cannot come out at work. Most people make jokes about it which is having catastrophic consequences on my life. It has made me have a bad fear about the whole thing." (Stock control clerk)

"I am now less inclined to come out at work. Due to wrong information on AIDS I think students (and staff) would react in a way which may present discipline problems in the classroom." (Lecturer, Further Education College)

"Whilst I would be quite open about my sexuality if anyone were interested, because of AIDS I think one becomes more reserved. In my profession I expect people to assume I'm gay!" (Interior designer)

"I have been working with children for four months so I feel that people who might otherwise accept my being gay could be swayed by media hysteria." (Nurse)

Hostility, jokes and snide remarks

"I fear a negative reaction to homosexuality because of the media distortion of AIDS." (Civil servant)

"Although my being gay was more or less an open secret at my last office, I do feel that the general media hype about AIDS has created a hostile atmosphere for gays which will continue to exist until AIDS itself is more generally understood." (Unemployed)

"There was a blood transfusion unit at work. Everybody gave blood except me and it was noticed! The other workers are hostile to gays and the AIDS issue." (Local Government Officer)

"Since AIDS there has been more hostility, more anti-gay jokes etc. More stigma attached to being gay." (Civil servant)

"I got snide comments until I took the leaflets on AIDS into work and handed them out." (Civil servant)

"Since the advent of AIDS there's been a lot of 'watch that mug' and that kind of thing. Just the other day somebody came and said to the director 'Sorry, the cup's cracked'. He said 'Oh, I don't think I'll get AIDS from it ... know what I mean Tim?'" (Actor)

"There are jokes made about it. I was ill earlier this week and somebody said, 'Are you sure it's food poisoning?'. It was a joke but I think there may have been something behind it." (Residential social worker)

"Even though I work among health care personnel they make ill-informed statements about getting AIDS from gay patients." (Nurse)

"Somebody I work with, who was always very physical towards me, now always offers her cheek to kiss instead of her mouth. I think people's understanding of AIDS is very limited. They seem to get their information from the press, picking up the general hysteria." (Actor)

Sacked

Gay men have been sacked from their jobs because of AIDS hysteria. In Barry's case, quoted below, the people he worked with seemed to be good mates until AIDS hysteria changed their attitudes towards him — attitudes which led to him being sacked.

Barry (Storekeeper)

"Before I moved to London I worked in Scunthorpe for a sort of family business. My family knew the business and let out that I was gay. The people I worked with were all right about it and now and again we had a good laugh about it. No one had heard about AIDS at that time. Later it all got a bit too much, two of the blokes there had just started a family and I started getting comments about AIDS, 'You can't come and see my kid...' and all the rest of it. The man who took the company over brought some of his own family into it. They treated me like a lump of shit. So, I thought well my best plan is to move to London where most of the gays are. I thought if people in London knew I was gay then they wouldn't react like the people did in Scunthorpe.

I was on the dole for a while, looking for a job. The job came up in Smithfield Meters, a factory in Streatham. The money was good, quite a lot of holidays and shut down pay, bonuses and everything. At the interview they told me that people would be sacked for racist behaviour and I thought well that's good it means that they'll probably be all right about me being gay as well.

When I went into the factory I didn't say I was gay. I was positively sure I wasn't going to tell them, because of the trouble at the last job. The trouble is it means living two lives and I couldn't do it. I lasted quite a few months without telling them but girls there started trying to pick me up, asking me where I went at night and did I have any girl friends etc. So I got them all together and all the storage blokes, and told them I was gay. Then I just left them to think about it. They came up and told me afterwards that they thought I was brave to come out in front of about 20 straight people and tell them I was gay.

After that we had a few laughs and people would ask me questions about my way of life. When they saw things in the paper they asked me questions. I always told the lads when they talked about AIDS that the only way they would catch it, even if I had got it, was to go to bed with me. I told them I didn't fancy them! Then later on the lads read in the paper about a woman who had caught AIDS. The article said that the woman was nursing an AIDS victim and she had eczema and small cuts on her hand and caught it without sexual intercourse. Things just flared up from there. They thought if that woman could catch it then they could.

They went to management and said that they were scared of catching AIDS. I'd told them that I'd got mates who were antibody positive but they knew I was negative because I'd told them. I even got the clinic to write it down to prove it. They never said anything to me about it but they told management that they wouldn't work with me or the stuff that I was touching. I didn't know it was going on until this person came up and put a sticker on me which we used for certain things we worked with saying 'Keep In Quarantine'. They stuck it on my back and I took it off and said 'What's this for?' He said you've got to keep in quarantine, keep away from all us lot. It upset me at the time because I'm having problems at home as well. I can't go home at Christmas because they're scared of getting AIDS as well.

I went up to see a man about it who works for that department and asked him what I could do, I didn't want to get anyone into trouble, so I didn't want to go any higher. He said other problems could be sorted out but not this one, so I ought to go and see the management. So I went to see a director and apparently the others had already been to complain. He said 'Well, I'm glad you've come to tell me because it's a difficult subject to bring up and I'm glad you've brought it up. We'll let it rest a bit, see if the trouble goes down a bit and go from there.'

I suppose between then and when I went to see him the day after, the director had gone down to see personnel. I think he'd talked it over with another director and a doctor. The doctor said he couldn't tell the others for definite that they wouldn't get AIDS even though I was negative. The directors decided that the only way to solve the problem was to get rid of me. That's how it came about that I was sacked.

After that I was offered full-time work at a gay pub. I thought about it. It wasn't much money, but I took it. There aren't many gay jobs but I'm worried that if I went back into a straight job, it'll all happen again. Before I knew I could work at the pub full-time I went into job centres and there was quite a few advertised that I could do, good money as well, but I just couldn't go up to the counter and say I want this."

Leaving of free choice
For some gay men the AIDS hysteria has made their work environment so unbearable, they have decided to leave.

Brian (Schoolteacher)
"Last February I'd finished a relationship and was having a difficult time emotionally at home. So, as anyone might do, I went to workmates for support. For once, instead of being the butt of jokes about being gay, I was actually saying, 'I'm having problems at the moment. I need your support.'

Shortly after, I wasn't allowed to go into the toilets opposite the staff room. They suddenly designated it a women's only toilet. I'd been there for a year and a half by then and it never had been before. I said, 'What's all this?' and they said, 'Oh well it always has been a women's toilet and under health and safety we decided it should be back as a women's toilet'. I thought nothing of it at that point, and then I found out that two women members of staff were frightened that they would catch AIDS from me. They assumed that now I was a 'free agent' that I was going around sleeping with anybody or everybody. Therefore, they assumed that I was a potential carrier. I found out that was the reason for the toilet's re-designation.

On top of that, the same two staff started bringing in their own mugs. Their excuse was that they suddenly didn't like the school mugs because they were really filthy and dirty. I thought well all right, but they've been like that for years, why this sudden hygiene kick. Very rarely do I lose my temper but I actually lost my temper. Even the children noticed I was in a foul mood, which undermined my professional standing. There was another member of staff who was gay and he also found it offensive. Everybody else just said you're over-reacting, just calm down. 'I said nobody, but nobody, has that attitude about me and gets away with it. I'm leaving this hell hole.'

The headmistress got to hear about it and she hauled me in and said, 'I think you're being very unprofessional'. I said, 'Well I think they are, because as far as I'm concerned they are colleagues that need to ask me if they don't understand'. The headmistress decided that we would have to have a staff meeting about it. Before that, the other gay teacher decided that we should get the staff some fact sheets about

AIDS from the Terrence Higgins Trust to read. I gave one to everybody including the helpers.

We had a staff meeting and the headmistress chaired it. Her attitude was she could understand why I was offended and it was probably tactless on their part, but I must understand that they have others to consider at home, their family and friends. I thought wait a minute I may not have someone to consider, i.e. a lover or what have you, but my mother would be upset if I dropped down tomorrow and a few others too! I took great umbrage at that and so did the other guy. He actually went to somebody in the gay teachers group, and somebody else off the record in ILEA. Basically they said there was nothing that could be done unless we were willing to make a formal complaint. We talked and talked about it but decided that a formal complaint in that climate at that time would have been very dangerous. Possibly now when there's more information about AIDS we could have done. I think most of the members of staff and the parents knew I was gay but I don't think they knew he was.

After a few more incidents I got on to the phone to divisional office and said professionally I'm feeling stifled. I want to go to a school where I feel I can teach a wider age range and so on. But I think she found out why I wanted to leave."

Informing people about AIDS — the responsibility of gay men?
Many of the gay men interviewed said they had found that they alone had to inform people about the real facts about AIDS. It seems to have become the responsibility of gay men to be fully informed about every aspect of AIDS so that they can counter misinformation from the media.

Terry (Nurse)
"The subject of AIDS has come up once or twice, but I feel that there are people who are frightened to talk about it. When people have seen television programmes they may discuss it and say how hysterical it is, but at the same time they are the very people who have been reading 'The Sun', 'The Star', and the latest 'Shock! Horror!' headlines and they react to that. So on one level they try to be intelligent about it and on another level of emotion and prejudice they react in a separate way."

Ken (Librarian)
"People at work seemed to assume that because I was a gay man I'd be some sort of expert on AIDS. Every story that came up in the news and so forth, I was expected to comment on. They asked in a very nice, casual way and I gave as much information as I could. I felt towards the end of it, however, that it was a question of lumping all gay men and AIDS together.

I felt that if the media hadn't represented what was going on so badly, then, I wouldn't have to answer these questions. What worried me was that if I hadn't been there, or if there wasn't an out gay man on the premises, then all the straight working population would just come to their own conclusions. Not having a gay man to answer questions

Educating colleagues about AIDS.....

41

they'd just end up agreeing with the media or whatever it put forward. So I spent a lot of time refuting things and saying 'no, the problem is this…' or 'it's only contracted by that…' but I resented it slightly."

Kevin (Residential social worker)
"The only form of information that I have seen on AIDS has been from NALGO. One thing that concerned me was that the day we received about two dozen leaflets, after about fifteen minutes someone threw them in the bin. I picked them up and left them back where they were before. As far as I know, most of the staff read them, although what they took from them I don't know."

Michael (Punch operator with the DHSS)
"There has been a lot of stupid idiotic comments going about AIDS. For instance, LAGER sent me a fact sheet on AIDS and I mentioned it to someone in the office. Another person that was in the office at the time turned round and said, "I don't really want to read that" and walked out … in a way that wasn't just a passing comment. Another person wanted to wear rubber gloves across the counter because they take it that anybody who signs on is gay and therefore has AIDS! Someone else turned round and said we should have stricter measures because otherwise there was a likelihood of catching AIDS through touching claimants, using the same pens or materials as the claimants when you sign them on. Stupid comments that some of the newspapers breed about if you touch something a gay person has touched you immediately catch AIDS whether they've got AIDS or not. Complete ignorance.

The larger majority of my benefit office is fairly open about AIDS. They'll talk to me about it and they will actually want to know what the facts about AIDS are. When I started there, there was a hell of a lot going about AIDS in the newspapers. Stupid comments about catching it off toilet seats, touching or kissing a person and you'll get it. When I first went into the office they were ignoring it except for the minority. Nevertheless, it's usually up to me to tell people at work about the facts on AIDS. On the straight scene there isn't a lot of information about it. The press are using it as a scare tactic, a tactic to bring up prejudice against gay people.

I blame my union for a lot of the lack of information 'cos they haven't actually turned round and said 'This is what AIDS is about'. They haven't written anything in their newsletters or their newspapers. They haven't informed people of AIDS to the extent that they should.

I think if the union was to print a few more pieces about AIDS and if the Civil Service as a whole didn't have such a damn stupid attitude towards gay people it would be better all round. It could be taken up by unions and by management but they really don't give a damn. I mean they've let this go on, instead of reassuring people they have not reassured people."

Gary (Voluntary sector worker)

"I think a lot of people at work tend to believe what is said on the news about AIDS and have a lot of strange ideas about how AIDS can be contracted. At work I'm in a fortunate position where I can actually argue or discuss with them what points they've got and why they are wrong and a lot of other people can't do that.

I think people in all industries are being discriminated against and I think that the thing about AIDS is just being used as a sort of front. I think those people's prejudices have always been there. I don't think that AIDS has got anything to do with it. I just think people can be more openly hostile."

Tackling ignorance

It should not be the sole responsibility of gay men to inform people about AIDS. Employers and trade unions have a role to play to counteract AIDS hysteria. Some, albeit few, trade unions have taken the initiative to inform their members about AIDS. NALGO has been the most active in this sphere.

The educational system is a crucial medium for the dissemination of information. Quoted below is an example given by Alex of the initiative one headmistress took to inform her school about AIDS. The ILEA could develop a strategy to be incorporated into the school curriculum along the lines of this example.

Alex (Lecturer)

"A student on teaching practice last year ran into some nasty attacks at school, mostly about AIDS. He went to the deputy head and told her he thought he would have to leave and why. She said 'I'm not going to have that' and ran a superb counter attack throughout the school. She took assembly herself and talked about AIDS. She also asked the biology staff to spend a bit of time with every class explaining as much as they could about AIDS. She herself went to the classes where the worst attacks were coming from and had it out with them. The student stayed."

The danger of the antibody test

We pointed out earlier in the chapter that there is no test publicly available for the HIV virus. A test which is available at STD (Sexually Transmitted Diseases) clinics is a test for antibodies to the virus in the blood. The only thing a positive result to the test can tell you is that you have been in contact with the virus at some time. A negative result to the test does not, however, mean that you have not been in contact with the virus. Basically the test doesn't tell you anything!

The very existence of the test has caused difficulties for gay men. There are cases where employers have put pressure on gay male employees to take the test. There are cases where gay men have been asked to take the test during a medical before starting a job. Some gay men who have informed their employers that they are antibody positive have been sacked or asked to resign. To date there has not been an industrial tribunal case to test whether or not sacking someone for being antibody positive is upheld by law. Thus, no precedent has been set.

On a personal level finding out that you are antibody positive can be pretty devastating, even if you know it doesn't mean anything! There follow just a few examples of how taking the test can lead to difficulties.

Employers and the test
Martin (Trainee manager)

"I know of a case where a gay man was going to have 'the test' and wanted time off work. His supervisor called him and said he was suspended on full pay until he got the results from the hospital. His employers phoned up the hospital and the hospital told them about 'the tests'. So there was a breach of confidentiality from the hospital's point of view and a breach of moral something by the employers . Another example of someone having trouble at work because of taking the test is a nurse who is antibody positive. He told his employers he was antibody positive because he thought he had a duty to do so. They immediately got him to resign." (The Royal College of Nursing is looking into the case.)

Tim (Actor)

"Since the advent of AIDS, the screen actors guild has passed a resolution saying that if the part played involves kissing scenes then the actors involved must be tested for HTLV III antibody before they get their contract. It's an American guild although it may apply here."

Personal consequences
Ben (Occupation not stated)

"I had the test because I felt guilty and neurotic. I was swept up by all the media hype into thinking that everyone who was gay was bound to be marked by this contagion. I started looking for symptoms and found that I had a swollen gland in my neck. I was told that there was nothing wrong with that but I worried about it and eventually took the HIV test. I found I was positive. It's part of my personality that drove me to have the test. The only good thing about having the test is that I'm now more aware of that part of my personality, and I'm making attempts to control it.

The effect of finding out that I was positive was like a slow burn. I had to wait a month for the result. Although the consultant was very optimistic, saying that nine out of ten people with HIV are okay and so forth, there is still that nagging doubt that you are going to be part of the ten per cent.

I feel that what gay men should be doing is assuming that any of us could be positive, and behaving with responsibility and safe sex. So, if you are wondering whether or not to have the test, I'd say no. Assume that you are positive anyway. If you had the test and found out you were negative then you should still carry on with safe sex because the next person you go with could make you positive.

I don't really think that there is anything to be gained by taking the test. I think it causes you a lot of worry. The smallest pimple becomes something to worry about. I think the thing to do is to concentrate on being healthy. It's now a year and a half since I had the test and things are at last coming into perspective. For a time it was the first thing I thought about when I woke up in the morning and it just went on and on in my head. It was a state of extreme anxiety. Stress, of course, is supposed to lower your immunity so that can't be very good, can it!

At first I told some people I was positive, but now, apart from my immediate close family and friends, I don't tell anybody because of the hysteria involved. You hear about people who have said they are positive at work and the kind of adverse reactions they have had."

POINTS AND RECOMMENDATIONS

A tool for discrimination

Discrimination against gay men has increased and become more overt because of AIDS hysteria. AIDS is not a gay disease, to assume a gay man has AIDS adds a further stereotype to the many that already exist. Discrimination as a consequence of AIDS or AIDS hysteria is inextricably linked to homophobia and heterosexism. The fact that lesbians, the group most unlikely to catch AIDS, have suffered discrimination due to AIDS hysteria is clear evidence of the way AIDS has been used as a tool for heterosexism. In a great many cases AIDS has been used as an excuse to express prejudice against lesbians and gay men that already existed. AIDS has not only been used to discriminate against lesbians and gay men. The West German Government, for example, has used AIDS as an excuse for racism against people from the African continent. Students from developing countries who have received scholarships from the German Development Ministry are now required to take the HIV antibody test before they are allowed to take up their studies. The Times Higher Educational Supplement reported in December 1985 that the Federal Ministry for Economic Co-operation has:

> ...already sent back nine people from East and Central Africa who were found to have HTLV III antibodies in their blood.

No one should ever be forced to take the HIV antibody test, but it is clearly discrimination that students from developing countries *alone* should be subjected to the test.

It is not new or uncommon for a disease to be used as an excuse to discriminate against minority groups. Lorraine Trenchard makes this point...

> Throughout history, there have been many attempts to link diseases with various racial groups or classes. When there is an epidemic the people who have power often find it useful to scapegoat these groups. Oppressed groups are blamed and hatred is fanned. TB amongst the working classes of Victorian England and typhoid amongst the black communities of England's colonies are two obvious examples. These groups are not seen as victims, but are blamed for the diseases.[5]

The need for information

The public have been misinformed about AIDS mainly through the media. The

45

wrong information given by the press needs to be counteracted. Some recent newspaper articles and television programmes have tried to give a more informed view of AIDS. They are not enough to counter the sensationalism that much of the media still uses to report AIDS.

AIDS is a major public health problem. People need to be informed about the true facts of how it can and cannot be transmitted. Members of gay communities have been fighting for over five years for preventive measures to be taken, and information provided by the government to help stop the spread of AIDS. In March 1986, the Department of Health launched a £2,000,000 AIDS information campaign telling people how to avoid the virus. The campaign, although long overdue, was a move in the right direction. However, there is still much more that needs to be done to educate people about AIDS. One area badly in need of expansion is information and detail about safe sex. It is of great importance that information about safe sex is directed to everybody, not only to gay men. General information and information about safe sex should also be produced for people who do not read English and for people with visual disabilities.

Trade unions, employers and educational bodies
In addition to information about AIDS itself, there is a clear need for initiatives to be taken to counteract the increased homophobia that AIDS hysteria has generated. The government information campaign is unlikely to tackle this problem! Trade unions, employers and workers in education all have a role to play in this area.

Trade unionists have a duty to their members to ensure no one is discriminated against at work because of AIDS hysteria. From the experience to date gay men are the most likely to suffer discrimination caused by AIDS hysteria. The chapter on trade unions (Chapter 6) discusses the role that trade unions should be playing to fight against heterosexism and homophobia generally. Fighting AIDS hysteria by providing information to members and giving full support to any members who experience discrimination in relation to AIDS is an integral part of a general fight against discrimination.

Employers have a duty to be informed about AIDS. No one should be sacked from their job or harassed in any way because they are antibody positive. Equally no employer should assume that because an employee is gay, he therefore has AIDS. No employee should ever be forced to take the HIV antibody test. Employers/organisations who have or who are developing Equal Opportunities Policies (see chapter 5 page 49) should ensure that the policy is designed to fight against discrimination which occurs as a result of AIDS hysteria. In addition, it is important that conditions of service should be adapted to ensure that the right to compassionate leave is extended to lesbians and gay men. The need for compassionate leave to be extended to gay men has been highlighted by the advent of AIDS. It is important that employers are generous and sympathetic in their operation of compassionate leave for gay men who are caring for partners or close friends with AIDS.

The ILEA could devise an educational programme about AIDS for schools — an information programme which fights against AIDS hysteria and homophobia.

The NHS and health care

AIDS is already a major public health problem and one which is likely to grow unless more public money is invested into research to fight the disease. One of the ways in which discrimination occurs in the field of research itself is that areas which are apparently only relevant to a specific minority group are given inadequate resources for research.

The health service also needs more public money for the care and nursing of people with AIDS. In caring and nursing for gay men who have AIDS the health service should be aware of issues which are particularly relevant to lesbians and gay men. For example, the health service needs to understand the importance of friendship and support networks in lesbian and gay communities. It is usually not appropriate for the health service to use narrow definitions of "next of kin" or family to decide who should and should not be included in the caring, nursing and decision-making needed for gay men who are seriously ill as a result of AIDS

Personal advice

For anyone who is thinking of taking the HIV antibody test our advice is not to, without at least phoning the Terrence Higgins Trust first to discuss it.

To anyone who has had the test our advice is not to tell your employer. It's none of their business. Even if the results of the test are negative, you may find that your employer wants you to take the test again at a later date.

■ Chapter Five
Equal opportunities

Providing equal opportunities means ensuring that people from all groups in the community are employed and fairly represented throughout an organisation. It also requires that employees or users of the organisation are not discriminated against by other employees or by the structure of, and procedures used by the organisation. The adoption of an Equal Opportunities Policy (EOP) by an employer or organisation is both a recognition that discrimination exists within the organisation and an attempt to fight it.

This chapter begins with the results of the questions about Equal Opportunities in the survey of gay men and employment. It goes on to suggest guidelines for the development of Equal Opportunities Policies which include comments and ideas from the gay men responding to the questionnaire, and those who were interviewed face-to-face. The chapter ends with information about London local authorities and their policies to date.

The survey results

116 of the survey respondents said that their employer was an equal opportunities employer (58 per cent overall). This high proportion is a reflection of the large proportion of respondents who work in the public sector (51 per cent overall), particularly those who work for local authorities (38 per cent overall).

The content of Equal Opportunities statements and policies varies widely with different employers/organisations. Some employers give only vague statements of intent to "appoint the right person to the job", whereas a few employers have adopted comprehensive policies with measures to implement and monitor them. A comprehensive policy identifies the different forms of discrimination to be fought by the policy. Only 40 respondents (20 per cent) said that their organisation specifically mentioned lesbians and gays or sexual orientation in job adverts or other literature they produced. Most of these respondents worked in Labour-controlled local authorities or the GLC. The GLC and some Labour-controlled local authorities have been the forerunners in adopting comprehensive EOPs.

69 per cent of our respondents said they thought that Equal Opportunities Policies were effective. However, an even higher proportion thought that there was more that their own employer could do. 70 per cent of those who said that their employer already had an Equal Opportunities policy, and 77 per cent of those whose employer did not, said that they thought their employer could do more for Equal Opportunities.

"I work in the housing department which along with one or two other departments has a much more 'liberal' attitude towards equal opportunities. However, I have worked in areas of the council where I didn't feel easy enough to be open about being gay. These sections/departments exist everywhere and the situation is probably even more difficult for manual workers as they tend to work in more isolated situations." (Local government officer, Camden)

GUIDELINES FOR POLICIES

The guidelines below are given to aid employers, trade unionists, and any groups or individuals who are trying to establish or fight for comprehensive Equal Opportunities Policies.

Every EOP will differ according to the structure and type of organisation in question. The following guidelines can be used as a framework from which individual policies can be developed. Although the guidelines concentrate on the measures needed to combat discrimination which people experience because they are lesbian or gay, it is essential that policies are not designed with the assumption that all lesbians and gay men are white, middle class, non-Irish gentiles, without disabilities.

> It cannot be presumed that a policy designed to combat discrimination at work against a white gay man will have any effect on discriminatory practices against black lesbians. (Moreover, white gay men themselves are not innocent of racism and sexism.)[1]

Defining the content

The content of an EOP should include a general policy statement. The statement should declare that the employer/organisation operates an Equal Opportunities Policy and state which groups are covered by the policy. It is important that the policy statement affirms positive action and commitment to fighting discrimination. A good example of a comprehensive policy statement is that issued by the London Borough of Haringey...

> This Council declares its intention to become an equal opportunities employer. The council is opposed to discrimination on any grounds. In particular, we oppose discrimination on the grounds of race, colour, nationality, ethnic or national origin, sex, marital status, age, religion, and discrimination against lesbians and gay men, the unemployed and people with disabilities. The aim of our policy is to prevent racism, sexism, heterosexism, age-ism and other forms of discrimination against people from these groups, and to take affirmative action to ensure that they are represented as employees in all departments and at all levels. In particular, we are committed to action to ensure that the ability and potential for the job are the only criteria, and that this Council through all policies and actions does achieve an accurate reflection in its workplace of the community it serves.

Lesbians and gay men should be mentioned by name in the policy statement as opposed to the term "sexual orientation". Everybody has a sexual orientation and therefore the term does not name the people oppressed. Even if sexual orientation is assumed to refer to same sex relationships it still fails to distinguish between lesbians and gay men as different groups which suffer from oppression.

The policy statement should be widely advertised to all members of staff and to the public served (if applicable) by the organisation. The statement, or a summary version, should accompany all job advertisements. Job advertisements should be placed in newspapers and magazines which are relevant to the groups to which the policy is directed.

Ken (librarian)

"If I see a job advert which mentions lesbians and gay men, I automatically feel that there won't be any problems there and I would certainly apply for it. If I didn't see it then I would have to weigh it up. It would depend on the job and where it was and which local authority."

The development of policy

A general statement of commitment must be followed by a comprehensive EOP. The EOP should detail the specific strategy to be employed to fight each form of oppression identified in the policy statement. Although a strategy is needed to overcome each form of oppression it should be taken into account throughout the policy statement that all forms of oppression are inter-linked and interacting.

Protection in employment

Kevin (Residential social worker)

"Officially in my job I could be fired for being gay. When I actually sit down and think about that it's a cause for concern, it's unfair. While not being conceited I know I'm damn good at my job. I know I can do the job and I have absolutely no interest sexually in young children or teenagers. In any of my work there has been no reason for anyone to point a finger at me and say that there is a scandal and never has been. So, therefore, I don't see why I should be in a 'risk' area, which I am."

There is no law to prohibit employers from discriminating against employees because they are lesbian or gay. (Discussed in more detail in the chapter on gay workers and the law.) In the absence of legislation it remains the responsibility of employers and trade unions to ensure protection for lesbians and gay men in their jobs. An effective EOP can provide such protection.

The provision of an EOP by an employer/organisation is important not only to existing employees, but also to potential employees. Michael, for example, describes how the lack of an EOP for lesbians and gays at the DHSS made him think twice about applying.

"When I was unemployed I was dubious in even applying for jobs in the Civil Service because I knew what their views were about lesbians and gay men. I always wanted to be in the Civil Service but their views put me off. If they did include us in the equal opportunities scheme then there would be a lot more chance for lesbians and gays."

Protection in employment involves securing the right of lesbians and gay men to be open in their jobs and to be free from harassment. Condemnation of heterosexist harassment should be included in the EOP along with the condemnation of harassment through, for example, racism, sexism and harassment against people with disabilities. Harassment should be included in the conditions of service as acts of misconduct to be dealt with under disciplinary and grievance procedures.

Martin (Trainee manager, GLC)

"Rules and regulations are important and that there are structures you can go through, rather than having to fight all your own battles.

The GLC has helped not so much by leafleting, but by passing rules and regulations. It's all very well to say 'This is what you ought to be like', but to actually pass regulations and rules is, unfortunately, the best way."

Conditions of service

A complete and comprehensive review of the existing terms and conditions in an organisation is an essential aspect in the development of an EOP. The conditions of service which relate to particular jobs usually include pay, hours, benefits, and the employee's rights in relation to dismissal, redundancy and grievances.

Conditions of employment often discriminate against and ignore lesbians and gay men. For example, in our survey of gay men, only 21 respondents (11 per cent) said that their conditions included gay partners to be given benefits similar to those of married employees (including childcare). A few of the suggestions our respondents made for the way that conditions could be changed are as follows...

Totally overhaul all the conditions of service for heterosexist bias. (Trade union official)

Be more progressive in the recognition of homosexuality not only with leave in case of partners' illnesses but also in superannuation schemes. (Civil servant)

Practise equal opportunities and not just pay lip service. Introduce paternity leave regardless of sexual orientation as an equal opportunity. (Unemployed respondent)

Have a parity policy with regard to straight/lesbian or gay partners. (Post deliverer)

Equality of gay partners with spouses. (Civil engineer)

Allow me to nominate someone for pension benefits if I died and that person had been in some measure dependent on my pension or income. (Office worker)

Language and terms used in conditions of service often discriminate against lesbians and gay men. Conditions of service which relate to bereavement, compassionate leave and pension rights often exclude lesbians and gay men by defining relationships in heterosexual terms, terms such as husband/wife. Neutral definitions which can be used instead are, for example, "partners" and "dependants".

Recruitment and promotion

Whether or not a person is lesbian or gay should be irrelevant to their gaining a job or promotion. It should be recognised, however, that being lesbian or gay can be a positive contribution to an organisation. Jobs which involve dealing with the public, for example, ensure greater representation of that public if lesbians and gay men are included.

The procedures for recruitment and promotion need to be reviewed for an EOP to be effective. Many methods used for recruitment and promotion, particularly the use of interviews, personal records and references, are subject to the bias and prejudice of individuals. Interviews should be conducted to assess only a person's ability to do a job. Procedures used for interviews and on promotional boards should follow a standard plan devised to minimise personal bias.

Where possible short-listing and interviews should be conducted by a panel which is representative of all the groups in the community from which the employer recruits. Procedures used for interviews and promotion should be accountable to employers, trade unions and the interviewee.

References and personal records should be treated with caution. A bad reference may be the result of the personal prejudice of a previous employer. Personal records may report court cases which have only arisen because the law itself discriminates. The chapter on gay workers and the law, for example, describes how gay men can be convicted for offences for which there is no heterosexual equivalent. Employers should ignore such offences if they are recorded on personal records. Court cases which involve lesbians and gay men fighting for the custody of their children may also be recorded on personal records. Such cases are also irrelevant in considering employees for employment or promotion.

Implementation

Written policies on equal opportunities can be of little or no use unless measures are taken to ensure that the policies are put into practice. To be effective the policy must be fed through to all employees with explanation of the implications it has for each of them.

Training is an important aspect of implementation. Training should be conducted with the assistance of recognised trainers. A first training measure is to ensure that all employees are aware of the content of the EOP. Many procedures and programmes in an organisation will need to be modified or changed with the introduction of an EOP. Staff will need to be trained in the new methods and procedures being adopted. Training should be designed to encourage employees to challenge their own discriminatory attitudes and those of others. Training should also encourage awareness of the day-to-day heterosexism and homophobia that occurs in the workplace.

"Most of the problems which lesbians and gay men face in the kind of environment with which I am familiar arise from informal assumptions about what is normal and desirable. While an equal opportunities agreement would be welcome it would not begin to touch these assumptions. A commitment to oppose heterosexism in all the workings of Further Education would be necessary to make any significant change. Such a commitment seems a long way off." (Lecturer in Further Education)

"More needs to be done to educate everyone on their 'homophobic' tendencies. I feel I am being force-fed everything that is 'heterosexual and normal', i.e. the men ogling every woman that walks in the office, boasting about how many 'birds I pulled on Saturday night' etc. It needs to be shown how dangerous it is to enforce sexist views on all and sundry." (Telex operator)

A different area of training important for the implementation of an EOP is training for jobs. Many people who are discriminated against have suffered from a lack of opportunity to train for certain jobs. For example, women are often prevented or discouraged from training for jobs which have been traditionally performed by men. An effective EOP must devise methods to counteract such disadvantage. If equal opportunities are to be offered at all levels in an organisation, it is important that opportunities exist in training for jobs at all levels and in all departments. Training may need to be expanded and adapted for the successful implementation of an EOP, for example, providing courses which are targeted towards women and Black people.

Service delivery

An effective EOP should be of benefit not only to employees but also to all clients and customers served by the organisation. Thus, an important aspect of an EOP is to produce a specific document which details the policy and plan of action for service delivery. The document should be devised to explain how employees can operate the EOP in relation to their clients, users, and customers. For example, councils and organisations dealing with housing should ensure that lesbian couples and gay couples who require housing or re-housing are given the same priority as heterosexual couples. This includes recognising that lesbians and gay men may have children and other dependants to be taken into consideration.

Contract compliance
Most employers/organisations make financial transactions of some kind with other employers. An aspect of implementing an EOP is to encourage other employers to adhere to Equal Opportunities. Organisations often buy goods or services from other employers/organisations. Because of the Race Relations Act, the Sex Discrimination Act and Disabled Persons Act, employers can be required to show that their employment practices do not discriminate on the grounds of sex, race or disability. Employers cannot be required, but can be encouraged, not to discriminate against lesbians and gay men.

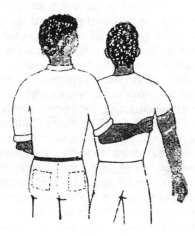

Monitoring and review
The final stage of an EOP is monitoring. Monitoring can ensure that policy development is an ongoing process. There are two main aspects of monitoring — first, ensuring that all groups in the community are being employed at all levels in the organisation; second, providing constant review of the content of the EOP. An EOP will need to be reviewed to incorporate any changes or developments which occur in an organisation.

Taking the initiative
Employers have often (if not always) needed to be encouraged to take lesbian and gay issues into account by lesbian and gay groups or individuals. Equal Opportunities Policies should be negotiated with relevant trade unions. This can be a help or a hindrance depending on the policies of the union concerned. Lesbian and gay trade union groups have often been the vehicle through which Equal Opportunities for lesbian and gay men have

been taken on board by employers and trade unions. This is not, however, the only way in which moves forward can be achieved. The following quotation gives an example of how a gay lecturer and students pushed for equal opportunities in their college.

Alex (Lecturer in Further Education)

"Just two years ago from now, I had been talking about inequalities at some length in a seminar. It was about gender, race and class, and how that was something we really ought to be concerned about. At the end of that seminar a student said, 'That's great and I agree with just about everything that's been said but there is one very substantial oppressed group that you have said nothing about and that's lesbians and gays.' I said, 'I'm gay and I totally agree with you.' He said 'Okay, what are we going to do about it?'

So in a way I was pushed forward, by what a student said to me. That was the year that we, a group of students and me, decided that we were going to push to get the whole question of 'orientation' onto the agenda. There was no opposition as such, except administratively, finding a place on the timetable and getting a space.

In that year we did two things: in the English department, a volunteer group, four students and me, prepared a whole resources pack and a whole morning's programme. We took it to the students and showed a video as well — they liked it very much. Much later in the year we got a morning for a whole course where about 400 people could have been there, but it was so late in the year that only 40 came. But we had official backing from the Post-Graduate Certificate in Education Course (PGCE). The newly appointed head of that course said that, 'I think that it's very, very important to do this.' He offered to speak.

The next year we said whatever happens we're not going to leave it to the end of the year. I found a space on the timetable in January for two hours, and set up a programme. 300 people came. Now, wherever equal opportunities appears on the course, then, as well as gender, class and race then the whole question of sexual orientation is supposed to come in. The important thing is that there has been no opposition except from a few students who in the meetings have voiced their fears or antagonism. But there has been no official opposition. Whether or not there is a type of hidden opposition I can't tell.

Our department has decided to appoint somebody called a consultant counsellor on equal opportunities. They have decided that I am to do it."

LOCAL AUTHORITIES

It was pointed out earlier in the chapter that some of the Labour-controlled local authorities and the GLC have been forerunners in the adoption of comprehensive EOPs. The adoption of EOPs by local authorities is crucially important. Within most London boroughs, especially those with high unemployment, local authorities are the largest single employers. Also local authorities provide services which affect every person living in the borough and should be representative of all the groups in the community they serve.

In the course of the research we wrote to every London borough to ask if they had an Equal Opportunities Policy or Policy statement. Those which did were asked to give detail of the content of the policy or statement. Only 11 of the 32 London boroughs replied.[2] The boroughs which did not reply to the letter were contacted by telephone. On the telephone we asked only if the borough had an Equal Opportunities Policy and if yes, did the policy specifically mention lesbians and gay men.

The plan below shows which London boroughs include lesbians and gay men in their EOP or Policy statement. More detail on the EOPs/Policy statements of the boroughs which replied to the letter are given in Appendix II.

The London Boroughs

1 Hounslow	6 Camden	11 Newham
2 Richmond upon Thames	7 Islington	12 Greenwich
3 Ealing	8 Haringey	13 Lewisham
4 Hammersmith	9 Hackney	14 Southwark
5 Brent	10 Waltham Forest	15 Lambeth

 Borough has an equal opportunities statement or policy which specifically mentions lesbians and gay men or sexual orientation

 Policy does not mention lesbians and gay men presently but policy is being negotiated

SUMMARY OF GUIDELINES

Although an EOP will differ with the type and structure of organisation, a basic framework can be followed which revolves around content, implementation and monitoring.

Content

The content of an EOP should include a general policy statement which declares that the employer/organisation operates an equal opportunities policy. The statement should state which groups are covered by the policy. The terms "lesbians and gay men" should be used in the statement as opposed to the terms "sexual orientation" or "sexual preference".

The general policy statement should be followed by a comprehensive Equal Opportunities Policy. The policy should detail specific strategy to be employed to fight each form of oppression identified in the policy statement. It is essential that throughout the policy it is taken into account that all oppression is inter-linked and interacting.

Lesbians and gay men have no protection in their jobs under employment law. An effective EOP gives protection to lesbians and gay men by ensuring their right to be open at work and to be free from harassment. Harassment should be included in conditions of service as an act of misconduct to be dealt with under disciplinary and grievance procedures.

Existing conditions of service should be comprehensively reviewed to ensure they apply equally to lesbians and gay men as to heterosexuals. Bereavement and compassionate leave are examples of conditions of service which often discriminate against lesbians and gay men by the language used, for example, by referring to husbands and wives. Neutral terms which can be used instead are dependants and partners.

The procedures used for recruitment and promotion often need to be changed when an EOP is put into operation. The use of interviews, personal records and references are all subject to the prejudice of individuals unless methods are devised to overcome such bias.

Implementation

Making the policy work is crucial. All employees (including management) and users of an organisation should be made aware of the content of the policy and the implications it has for them. An important aspect of implementation is training. There are two main areas of training required. First, training to ensure that all employees are aware of the policy content and how it is to be put into operation. Training should include the relevance of the policy to the day-to-day working environment. Second, the provision of training courses aimed to counter the lack of opportunity many people have suffered in the educational system and in subsequent employment.

Monitoring and review

An EOP must be constantly reviewed to be adapted to every change which occurs in an organisation. Monitoring is needed to ensure that all groups in the community are represented in an organisation at all levels.

∎ Chapter Six
Trade unions

TRADE UNIONS

This chapter concentrates on lesbian and gay issues in relation to the trade union movement. In the course of the chapter Equal Opportunities Policies (EOP's) are mentioned many times because we believe that all trade unions should be adopting comprehensive policies and encouraging employers to adopt them. To avoid too much repetition of the last chapter we have tried to concentrate on particular measures that trade unions can take in developing EOP's. These measures should be considered in conjunction with the general guidelines set out in chapter 5.

DISCRIMINATION — A TRADE UNION ISSUE

An important effect of discrimination in the labour market is that people are denied access to jobs because of their age, sex, race, religion, marital status, being lesbian or gay and people with disabilities. As a consequence people from discriminated groups suffer disproportionately from unemployment and are often forced to take jobs at the low paid end of the labour market. Trade unions should regard the provision of equal opportunities as a key issue in their fight for the right to work. It is partly because of the complacency that the trade union movement has shown towards issues of discrimination that employers are able to continue discriminating.

Trade unions exist to defend and protect the interests of their members. On the principles of equal treatment and fairness trade unions have a duty to ensure that the interests of all their members are taken into account. Too often trade unions still hold on to traditional and conservative notions that the "worker" is a white, heterosexual, male who is the "breadwinner" supporting a wife and children. Such a view relies on traditional notions of family and community which are not appropriate to contemporary Britain. Trade unions need to be aware of the interests of all groups in the community. They should ensure that all their members are protected in their jobs and free from harassment from employers and co-workers.

Ultimately it is in the interests of all workers to fight against discrimination. Discrimination divides workers and can be useful to employers because of this. The NCCL booklet *Gay Workers: Trade Unions and the Law* makes this point.

> If employers can make a scapegoat of one individual or minority group, or better still if they can allow others to do it for them, then they are able to deflect the blame for working conditions from themselves to that scapegoat.

Trade unions can and should be a vehicle through which all types of oppression can be actively fought. Increasingly, but slowly, more and more unions are beginning to realise that discrimination is a trade union issue.

The discrimination that people face because they are lesbian and gay has usually been last on the agenda for trade unions to discuss — many unions still ignore the issue altogether. However, over the last ten years there has been a growing awareness within the trade union movement that lesbians and gay men do suffer from discrimination in un/employment. Several unions have now adopted statements of no discrimination against lesbians and gay men and a few have developed policies aimed to actively fight discrimination. An important recent development in the fight for recognition of lesbian and gay rights is that a resolution calling for equal opportunities for lesbians and gay men was passed at the Trades Union Congress (TUC) conference 1985. The resolution, put forward by the National Association of Probation Officers (NAPO) and seconded by the National and Local Government Officers' Association (NALGO), states…

> Congress reaffirms the need for trade unions to protect the interests of their members and to recognise that lesbians and gay men have not always had full protection.
>
> Until legislation exists to cover discrimination on the grounds of sexual orientation, employers will continue to discipline and dismiss employees on the basis of misinformation and prejudice, unless trade unions take action to stop them.
>
> Conference calls on all affiliated trade unions:
>
> 1. To campaign for legislation to protect lesbians and gay men against all forms of discrimination in all areas of life.
>
> 2. To include lesbians and gays in all negotiated equal opportunities clauses and agreements.
>
> 3. To raise awareness of the issues within their own organisation.
>
> 4. To examine terms and conditions of employment such as pensions, bereavement leave and caring for children and dependants, to ensure that no discrimination exists on the grounds of sexual orientation, and
>
> 5. To support openly members who are victimised as a result of their sexuality.

The passing of the above resolution means that it is now official policy of the TUC to adhere to the recommendations stated in the resolution. The TUC executive and each of the 89 trade unions affiliated to the TUC should be taking positive action to ensure that this policy is put into operation. To date our evidence suggests that it is only a relatively small number of trade unions which are taking positive action, but the success of passing the resolution itself should not be underrated.

Below is a list of those trade unions for which we are able to give some information concerning their position on lesbian and gay rights.[1] All of the unions listed which have an EOP which includes lesbians and gay men or sexual orientation also include race, sex and disabilities in their EOP.

ACTT (Association of Cinematograph, Television and Allied Technicians) — Policy includes lesbians and gay men. Lesbian and gay working party meets regularly to discuss issues.

BFAWU (Bakers, Food and Allied Workers' Union) — Letter received by LAGER from a BFAWU National Health and Safety Officer states "The Union is opposed to the discrimination of people at work due to their sexual orientation. Where any members were being discriminated against for this reason, the Union would strive to support and protect them".

CPSA (Civil and Public Services Association) — Have national policy which includes lesbians and gay men. Letter to LAGER states "We have regular contact with the Civil Service Gay Group and whenever their activists feel there is a need for discussion and/or assistance on issues arising from their work, we are only too prepared to help".

COHSE (Confederation of Health Service Employees) — Motion carried at COHSE conference to support work being done by the Gay Rights at Work committee.

EIS (Educational Institute of Scotland) — Passed motions which resolve that homosexuality should not justify dismissal or lack of promotion.

IPCS (Institute of Professional Civil Servants) — Include "sexual orientation" in their policy statement. Their Equal Opportunities Working Party has produced a paper on gay/homosexual issues. The paper has been cleared by the union and has now been taken to the Council of Civil Service Unions for discussion.

NAPO (National Association of Probation Officers) — Have national policy on lesbian and gay rights.

NALGO (National and Local Government Officers' Association) — Has national policy which includes lesbians and gay men. NALGO was the first union ever to add "sexual orientation" to its non-discrimination clause in 1976. Since 1976 it has carried out several initiatives aimed to counter heterosexism. Its work includes holding meetings and producing literature about lesbian and gay issues.

NATFHE (National Association of Teachers in Further and Higher Education) — National EOP includes lesbians and gay men. Recently (1986) produced discussion paper on sexual orientation which seeks to raise understanding of the educational and trade union issues attaching to sexual orientation.

NUJ (National Union of Journalists) — Includes "sexual orientation" in their EOP. The NUJ has an Equality Council and has recently established an Ethics Council. Both councils include lesbian and gay issues in their work. Considering the large number of racist, sexist and heterosexist articles which appear in our newspapers every day it would appear that the NUJ are having great difficulty in implementing their policies.

NUPE (National Union of Public Employees) — Have national policy statement which includes lesbian and gay rights. Have published leaflets and produced information about the discrimination of lesbians and gay men. At the time of going to press a comprehensive equal opportunities agreement is in the concluding stages of negotiation.

NUS (National Union of Seamen) — Letter received by LAGER from an NUS research officer states "The NUS upholds the rights of individuals not to be discriminated against on grounds of race, nationality, religion, sex or sexuality. This is the case on all aspects of employment."

SCPS (Society of Civil and Public Servants) — Passed a motion against discrimination on the grounds of "sexual orientation" (1980).

TGWU (Transport and General Workers' Union) — National policy includes lesbians and gay men.

Three points should be taken into account concerning the above list —
First, there may be other trade unions which specifically mention lesbians and gay men in their equal opportunities policy or statement but we have not received or been able to obtain information from these unions.
Second, there are unions which do not mention lesbians and gay men in their policies who might support employees who were sacked because they are lesbian or gay. For example, a letter received by LAGER from an HVA (Health Visitors Association) librarian/information officer makes no reference to policies or motions against discrimination of any kind but states...

> I am not aware of any members who have experienced difficulties in obtaining employment or promotion because of their homosexuality but the Association would, no doubt, support a member should a problem of this nature arise.

Third, the above list does not mention work that unions have done in negotiating equal opportunities agreements with employers. For example, the Civil Service unions at the Department of Education and Science have recently secured an agreement that sexual harassment on the grounds of sexual orientation will be considered a disciplinary offence.
At the time of going to press all the EOP's which trade unions have negotiated with employers have been at local level. That is, union officials at a branch or regional level negotiate with local employers to develop equal opportunities agreements or policies which include lesbians and gay men or "sexual orientation".[2]
The rest of this chapter looks at the trade union issues which arise from the results of the LAGER survey and the interviews with gay men.

SURVEY RESULTS
In the LAGER survey of gay men and employment, 112 respondents said they were a member of a trade union or a staff association (58 per cent of those who answered the question). Table 1 is a breakdown of the trade union membership of those respondents who stated who their employer was. From Table 1 it is clear that a far higher proportion of respondents who work in the public sector are members of a trade union than respondents who work for private employers. Only 42 per cent of respondents who work for the private sector are members of a trade union compared with 88 per cent of those who work for the public sector (i.e. respondents employed by Local Authorities, Government Departments and other public sector employers). The high

proportion of public sector employees who are members of a trade union is a reflection of general patterns of trade union membership. Trade unions which serve public sector employees tend to be large, highly organised unions.

TABLE 1
Trade union membership by employment sector
(Percentages in brackets)

Employer	Yes, a trade union member	Not a member	No answer	Total
Private Employer	22 (42)	28 (53)	3 (6)	53
Voluntary Sector	3 (50)	3 (50)	0	6
Local Authorities etc.	45 (90)	4 (8)	1 (2)	50
Government Departments	12 (86)	1 (7)	1 (7)	14
Other Public Sector	2 (67)	1 (33)	0	3
Other	2 (40)	3 (60)	0	5
	86 (66)	40 (31)	5 (4)	131

56 respondents did not state who their employer was. Those answering the question-naire as unemployed or students are excluded from the Table. The five respondents who are recorded in the table as giving no answer are respondents who gave their occu-pation but did not state if they were a trade union member or not.

THE INTERVIEWS AND ISSUES ARISING

Information

Many of the gay men who were interviewed face-to-face expressed the view that trade unions can play an important role in fighting discrimination against lesbians and gay men. Terry, for example, talked of the need for people to be informed.

Terry

"If unions do take up lesbian and gay issues it makes a difference because then it brings it up in people's minds. Most people don't think about gay issues. 'Gay' is something they read about on the front page of 'The Sun' if there's a scandal, otherwise it's a non-event. It doesn't exist around them at all. They don't know anybody who's lesbian or gay and it's something that happens in the centre of London — 'somewhere else'. When it's mentioned in the work place it brings it home to them that the people next door may be gay or the people around them, and those people may in fact be suffering oppression or prejudice that they don't know about."

People generally do not have access to information about lesbian and gay issues. Most of the information people do receive is from homophobic and sensationalist press reporting. If trade unions are going to ensure that all workers are given equal treatment by other union members then it is important for trade unions to provide information not only about lesbian and gay issues, but also about racism, sexism and discrimination suffered by people with disabilities. The information should include the union's policy statements on each form of discrimination and clear guidelines for the plan of action to be followed in order to implement each policy.

It is important that information is disseminated at all levels (including the NEC and all union officials) of the trade union. It should be remembered that on most occasions a shop steward will be the first union official who can be contacted by a union member who has a grievance or problem with their employer or co-workers. Any members who feel that they are being discriminated against because of racism, sexism, heterosexism or because they are people with disabilities, should be able to feel confident that their shop steward will have an understanding and be supportive of their claims. Another role of shop stewards involves negotiating pay and conditions with employers. Part of these negotiations should be to encourage employers to examine their terms and conditions of employment to ensure that they do not discriminate. Obviously, to achieve this shop stewards themselves must be fully informed of the types of changes required.

The methods of giving information need careful consideration. Leaflets, pamphlets and articles in newsletters are important ways of providing information to members but, unfortunately, can be easily ignored. It is very important that all union officials are encouraged not only to disseminate written information but also to discuss issues with other members. Conferences, meetings and workshops are all arenas where discussion can take place, but challenging discriminatory attitudes and beliefs in day-to-day work situations is equally important.

The chapter on EOP's mentions training as an important aspect of the implementation of an EOP. We recognise that it would be impossible for trade unions to provide awareness training for all members. However it should be the policy of trade unions to provide some type of awareness training for executive members about, for example, racism, heterosexism, sexism, disability and the links between all forms of oppression.

Lesbian and gay input
The trade unions which have developed policies or passed motions against the discrimination of lesbians and gay men have done so almost invariably because of the efforts of lesbian and gay members active in their union. It has often been a small group of lesbians and gay men who have put forward demands to their union. Gary, whose job in the voluntary sector involves working with trade unions, commented on the importance of lesbians and gay men being active in their union.

Gary
"I think that lesbians and gay men should try for positions such as shop stewards and be active members. In my work with trade unions I find that the places and unions branches that have knowledge and understanding of lesbian and gay issues tend to have open lesbians and/or gay men there."

Self organised groups

Increasingly lesbian and gay members of trade unions are organising themselves to form lesbian and gay groups (the present lesbian and gay trade union groups are listed under *Groups*, page 97). Trade unions should recognise lesbian and gay groups and their right to self organisation. Because of the entrenched heterosexism in the trade union movement it is crucial that lesbians and gays are able to formulate their demands without the interference of heterosexual members. Lesbian and gay groups should be able to organise and have an input at all levels within a trade union. This does not mean that heterosexual members should leave all the campaigning work against heterosexism to be done by lesbian and gay members!

A comprehensive EOP should include the right for all groups who suffer discrimination to be self organised. Thus trade unions should encourage self organised Black groups, women's groups, disability groups and lesbian and gay groups to exist along side all levels of union structure. The self organised groups should have a recognised input into union consultation processes.

NALGO has been the most progressive of all the unions in developing specific policy and strategy to fight discrimination against lesbians and gay men. Ken describes some of the recent progress that NALGO has made in implementing its policy.

"As of about nine months ago, the union had a very woolly sort of "Oh yes we don't mind what goes on" type attitude, the union was dominated until a few years ago by a lot of fairly right wing, white, middle class men. A lot of women's issues and Black issues and certainly lesbian and gay issues were just not touched on. But gradually that's all changed, there's been a lot of changes in the union management, and they … we are now just at the beginning of debate.

The women's group has got off the ground, the lesbian and gay group has just got off the ground. We've also appointed an equal opportunities officer, and he's done a report on all the different sections. We're just at the point of trying to get all our rules changed so that in the future on branch executives, which manage the union, there will always be representation from lesbians and gay men, women, people with disabilities and Black sections." [3]

Implementation

The unions which do have specific policy for lesbians and gay men vary enormously in the extent to which they implement their policies. All too often in the field of equal opportunities, unions are willing to adopt policy as a principle but resist measures to actively implement that policy.

Implementation is often very poor at branch level. It is often up to individual members of a branch to push for issues of discrimination to be discussed. Despite the fact that the CPSA *does* have a national policy for lesbians and gay men, Michael found he had to bring the issues to the attention of his union.

"I'm a union representative so I attend a lot of meetings. I felt my union had neglected lesbian and gay issues so last week when we had a meeting I brought up the issue of lesbians and gays myself. The response was like I'd dropped a bomb shell — they suddenly discovered that there was someone gay in their branch. I don't think that my branch of the CPSA have had an openly gay union rep for some time or even before — I don't know. It seemed that my branch did think that they had to do something when I said that I think that the gay issue had been pushed aside."

Male attitudes
Ken

"The majority of people I work with are women and they are very, very supportive because we have sort of common problems and aims. I get more support from them than I do from straight men within the system for various reasons."

It is still the case that most of the lesbian and gay groups which exist are in unions which represent public sector employees and white collar workers. In addition most of the unions which have developed policies for lesbians and gay men have a high proportion of women in their voting membership (although most of the executive members of these unions are still men). There has been little progress in the fight against sexism and heterosexism in unions which are dominated by men in their voting membership. This includes most of the unions which represent workers in areas of employment which have traditionally been considered "men's work", for example, engineering and construction. For lesbians and gay men who work in male dominated areas of employment it is often impossible to come out (see chapter on day-to-day work, page 23). The attitudes of heterosexual men often conform to a "macho" image or "cult of masculinity" which rely upon sexism and heterosexism to be sustained. Because many lesbians and gay men are not able to be open in male dominated areas of employment it is impossible for them to bring lesbian and gay issues to the attention of their union.

Trade union executives should not need pressure from members to develop equal opportunities policies. The executives should realise that they have neglected lesbian and gay issues and it is their responsibility as trade unionists to implement change. It is now the policy of the TUC to oppose discrimination against lesbians and gay men at all levels. Trade unions should be acting upon all the points put forward in the resolution.

Race

Several of the Black gay men interviewed expressed the view that shop stewards were often reticent to take on issues of racism. Trade unions generally were seen to be dominated by white people who largely ignored issues that are important to Black people.

A large number of trade unions do have either policies or policy statements against racism. The extent to which efforts are made to implement these policies varies enormously but it is still the case, even in unions with a high proportion of Black members, that the vast majority of trade union officials are white.[4]

Representation

People who are from groups which suffer discrimination should ideally be represented at all levels in union structure. The methods of ensuring representation of different groups within the union will depend on the structure and organisation of the union in question. Because of the many different ways in which trade unions organise it is impossible to lay down strict guidelines for each trade union to follow in order to achieve a fair representation of different groups. A comprehensive EOP should include a plan of action and targeting to change representation in trade unions.

Wherever possible unions should set up Equal Opportunities Units (some unions already have). Ideally these should exist at all levels in the union. The extent to which unions are able to set up such units will depend on size and resources. The role of an Equal Opportunities Unit is to develop and monitor the equal opportunities policy of a trade union and to make certain that it is being implemented. Part of this role should include laying down guidelines for the union to act upon in order to achieve representation of different groups throughout the union.

Combined efforts

Many times during this report we have tried to emphasise that the fight against lesbian and gay discrimination should be part of a fight against all types of discrimination. People who do suffer discrimination have more strength if we all support each other in our different but related struggles.

An example of the way in which lesbians and gay men have organised to support the struggles of others was in the 1984 miners' strike. Lesbians and Gays Support the Miners (LGSM) and Lesbians Against Pit Closures (LAPC) were set up specifically to support the miners and the women in the mining communities. Sam describes LGSM and the important effect it had.

"Lesbians and Gays Support the Miners was set up to collect money and give whatever support we could for the miners on strike in 1984. In doing so we were able to make contact with another group who were being oppressed — building bridges if you like. We didn't go to them and say 'You support us and we'll support you', because the main purpose of LGSM was to support the mining communities — but we did hope that this would also lead to them supporting us.

We collected money by going round lesbian and gay pubs, clubs and so on and held public meetings to inform or educate lesbians and gays about the importance of supporting the miners on strike. When we collected money we made sure that it was obvious who we were doing it for and why we thought lesbians and gay men should give their support. A 'Pits and Perverts' concert was also held and raised enough money to buy a minibus for the miners.

When the strike had started we made contact with the NUM and it was decided that one of the ways we would give money was to 'adopt' the Dulais Valley miners. The people in the valley invited a group of us down for a weekend. They were nervous about us coming and we were nervous about going! When we got there it was great, the myths they had about us and the myths we had about them seemed to break down.

Politically LGSM made a big impact on the trade union movement because it led trade unions to take notice of lesbian and gay issues. I don't think the motion to support lesbians and gays would have got through the TUC conference if it hadn't been for LGSM. I also think it was very important that LGSM was an autonomous support group. If individual lesbians and gays had just joined other support groups the lesbian and gay issue wouldn't have come up."

TUC resolution

The gay men interviewed were asked if they thought the resolution (see page 60) passed at the TUC would make a difference to their union (if they were a member) and to the trade union movement generally. Most of the gay men interviewed who were members of the trade union were optimistic about the fact the resolution was passed.

Martin

"The resolution must make a difference. You can have good intentions as much as you like, but until they are actually written down, in black and white, so people are forced to follow them, nothing will change. Even writing them down is not going to change things over night, but it is a hopeful sign. You can always fall back on rules and regulations and say 'Look, this is what has been voted and you've got no right to do whatever it is you're doing.'"

Gary

"I think the TUC decision means that gay people within the trade union movement have actually got an extra lever to try and put pressure on the unions nationally to accept a similar policy to the TUC one. I think it can be used to change union policy if it's done properly."

Ken

"I think, yes, it will make a difference. Because our union (NALGO) is guided by what the TUC does, and I always think branch unions get a bit frightened about being the first persons to do something, they all like to move along fairly carefully together — nobody wants to stick their neck out and certainly not in a union in a right wing council. I think given that sort of example by the TUC they will be more positive."

AIDS

The chapter on AIDS and related issues talked about the need for trade unions to inform members of the real facts about AIDS and to show how it is being used as a tool for heterosexism.

The attitudes that individual trade unions have taken towards issues related to AIDS in many ways parallel the attitudes that different trade unions have toward lesbian and gay issues. Martin, a volunteer worker with the Terrence Higgins Trust, commented on the response trade unions had made to a Trust conference (November 1985).

Martin

"The Trust is holding a conference in November, some unions have threatened to boycott it, yet other unions, NALGO for example, have brought out AIDS guidelines. Some unions are good, some are bad. We have written to all the unions but not one of them has written back and asked us to send someone to speak to them. Letters have come back on related issues, which the unions think are important, but which fall wide of the mark. We've had letters from the publicity people and from the top people in the unions but letters about the issues they worry about which are often not the ones they should be worried about."

In November 1985 the journal "Labour Research" contacted all the TUC affiliated unions asking for details of their publications/advice on AIDS for their members. 25 unions responded to their letter, and as would be expected, the health service unions had issued the most advice. The results of their research are printed in Appendix III.

It is important that trade unions develop and implement policies to ensure that their members are protected against AIDS-related discrimination. An example of the type of policy we recommend is set out in the following motion accepted by the TGWU as policy.

In view of the hysteria created by the media coverage of Acquired Immune Deficiency Syndrome (AIDS), this Region calls on the General Executive council to:

1. Recognise that any individual who has contracted AIDS, or whose relatives or partners have been exposed to the virus irrespective of source, require full support of this union. Also to ensure that no discrimination occurs against any such individual as the result of prejudice or ignorance about the syndrome or its means of transmission.

2. Reassure co-workers that this virus can only be transmitted by direct blood contact and that there is absolutely no risk of contracting AIDS from social contact, toilets, eating or drinking utensils.

3. Ensure that no discrimination occurs against members who are believed to be in a high risk category: gay men, medical conditions requiring use of syringes or blood products or transfusion of blood products, irrespective of sexuality.

4. Hold on-going education workshops on AIDS to inform all co-workers of the true nature and risks of the disease in a factual manner.

5. Protest to the press council and the Campaign for Press and Broadcasting Freedom on the biased media coverage of AIDS, especially the publication of names and addresses of those diagnosed as having the virus.

6. Demand that the government make extra funds available for investigation and treatment of AIDS, especially in the London district, since Health Authorities cannot carry out the necessary research from their already over-stretched resources.

POINTS AND RECOMMENDATIONS

Discrimination is a trade union issue. Trade unions have a duty to their members to ensure that they represent the interests of all discriminated groups in the community.

Over the last few years there has been a growing awareness in the trade union movement that discrimination is a trade union issue. However, although most trade unions have made at least vague statements of "no discrimination", many still fail to recognise the importance of developing policies designed to fight each form of discrimination.

Discrimination against lesbians and gay men has been ignored by many trade unions. Trade unions should take note that is now official policy of the TUC, and thus all affiliated unions, to *actively* fight discrimination against lesbians and gay men.

Each trade union should have a comprehensive EOP which details specific plans to fight discrimination on the basis of age, race, sex, religion, marital status, being lesbian or gay or people with disabilities. It is essential that when such policies are developed they are fully implemented and monitored at all levels in the union structure.

It is important that trade unions develop and implement policies aimed to protect and inform members against AIDS hysteria and related discrimination.

Trade unions should be encouraging employers to develop comprehensive equal opportunities policies which include lesbians and gay men along the lines set out in chapter 5.

All terms and conditions negotiated with employers should be scrutinised for heterosexual bias.

Trade unions should support the right of any member ot be openly lesbian or gay in their job. Any member who experiences discrimination by employers or co-workers because they are lesbian or gay should receive the full support of their union. However, in developing policy, trade unions must also recognise that many lesbians and gay men are discriminated against as a result of more than one form of oppression. Thus, some lesbians and gay men may regard another form of oppression as the primary way in which they are discriminated against, for example racism, and may choose not to be open.

Most of the information people have about lesbians and gay men is from sensationalist and inaccurate press reporting. Trade unions can help to counter this misinformation by providing information to members about lesbian and gay issues. Information should be disseminated at branch, regional and executive level.

Self organised lesbian and gay trade union groups should be recognised and have the right to exist at all levels in the union structure. The right to self organisation should exist for all groups who suffer discrimination.

Trade unions should be developing a strategy to ensure that groups who are discriminated against are represented as officials at all levels in the union structure, including executive level.

■ Summary of recommendations

GAY WORKERS AND THE LAW

Employment law

Under present employment law lesbians and gay men can be sacked, demoted or refused promotion simply because they are gay.

- The law needs to be changed to make discrimination against lesbians and gay men illegal.

- It is essential that a change in law designed to protect lesbians and gay men in employment mentions lesbians and gay men specifically and not sexual orientation.

Unfair dismissal

- In the interest of all employees, legislation which relates to unfair dismissal needs to be reviewed. Many of the rules and regulations involved in cases of unfair dismissal give an unfair bias to employers. For example, many employees are unable to fight their dismissal at tribunals because they have not worked for their employer long enough to qualify for a hearing.

- Any attempt to change the law to make unlawful the dismissal of lesbians and gay men on the grounds of sexuality must ensure that there is no minimum qualifying period of continuous employment before a complaint can be brought against an employer.

Composition of industrial tribunals

An examination of past cases involving the dismissal of lesbians and gay men reveals that industrial tribunal panels have, on several occasions, accepted reasons from employers which are blatantly heterosexist as "reasonable" grounds for dismissal. There is no obligation for tribunal panels to reflect employers or employees in terms of their race, sex, class, being lesbian or gay, or people with disabilities.

- The statutory requirements for the composition of industrial tribunals need to be changed. At the very least there should be a requirement that the lay members of the tribunal representing the employees' interests should reflect the applicant bringing the case in terms of race, sex, class, disability and/or being lesbian or gay.

- To achieve such aims there would have to be a pool of lay members available to sit on tribunals who represent a spread of all the discriminated groups in the community. This should be taken into account in future appointments to tribunal panels.

Appointments to tribunals

Lay members are appointed to industrial tribunal panels every three years by the Secretary of State for Employment and are nominated by sponsoring bodies. The sponsoring bodies which nominate lay members for the employees' side are the Trades Union Congress (TUC) and The Managerial, Professional and Staff Liaison Group (MPG).

- Trade unions should act to ensure that lesbians and gay men and all other oppressed groups are represented on tribunal panels. To be effective, the sponsoring bodies must develop a policy, worked out with relevant groups in the community, which seeks to ensure that the lay members nominated redress the existing imbalance on tribunal panels.

Sexual offences

Criminal law discriminates against gay men, and can have consequences for gay men in employment or looking for work.

- Employers and organisations must be made aware that sexual offences between gay men have no victims and exist only because the law discriminates against us.

- Many of the laws which discriminate against gay men are to be found in the Sexual Offences Acts of 1956 and 1967. These Acts need to be totally revised and changed to give equal status to gay men under the law. Particular aspects of the Act which need to be repealed are, for example, the sections which deal with gross indecency and importuning (Sexual Offences Act 1956 ss 13 and 32). The laws relating to the age of consent and privacy should be brought into line with equivalent heterosexual laws. Overall, the law should not deem unlawful any sexual contact between members of the same sex which is lawful between members of the opposite sex. The repeals and revisions should also apply to members of the Armed Forces.

Working with children

The system of disclosure of criminal convictions of those with, or wishing to have access to children is currently under review. One of the main purposes of the review is to extend the right of disclosure to all organisations whose work involves children (both statutory and voluntary bodies).

- It is essential that all organisations whose work involves access to children have a system of checking the suitability of employees or potential employees. The dangers of disclosure are, however, that convictions irrelevant to working with children may be considered to show an unsuitability for employment.

- It is important that a system of disclosure is devised which does not allow the personal prejudice of employers or consultative bodies to influence the decision to employ. A system could include, for example, statutory guidelines to be introduced to ensure safeguards against discrimination and to introduce an element of standardisation.

- A system of disclosure should be devised which ensures that only "correct" or "accurate" information is provided and that employees or job applicants can know what is disclosed and challenge it if it is wrong.

- Any dismissal based on incorrect information should be automatically unfair.

DAY-TO-DAY WORK

Individual responsibility

Lesbians and gay men experience the effects of discrimination both blatant and subtle, direct and indirect, in ordinary everyday work situations by employers, co-workers and the public they deal with.

- It cannot be stressed too strongly that although changes in the law and employment conditions and procedures are needed to fight against discrimination, individual attitudes must also change as part of the fight to eliminate heterosexism. Individuals who define themselves as straight, heterosexual or not lesbian or not gay, should examine and challenge their own actions, attitudes and beliefs and those of others.

AIDS

Discrimination as a consequence of AIDS or AIDS hysteria is inextricably linked to homophobia and heterosexism. In a great many cases AIDS has been used as an excuse to express prejudice against lesbians and gay men that already existed. In some countries AIDS has also been used as an excuse for racism.

- AIDS is not a gay disease, to assume a gay man has AIDS adds a further stereotype to the many that already exist.

Information about AIDS

- The public have been misinformed about AIDS mainly through the media. The wrong information given by the press needs to be counteracted. AIDS is a major public health problem and people need to be informed about the true facts of how it can and cannot be transmitted. Although the Department of Health has conducted an information campaign this needs to be expanded.

- One area badly in need of expansion is information and detail about safe sex. It is of great importance that information about safe sex is directed to everybody, not only to gay men. General information and information about safe sex should also be produced for people who do not read English and for people with visual disabilities.

Counteracting homophobia

In addition to information about AIDS itself, there is a clear need for initiatives to be taken to counteract the increased homophobia that AIDS hysteria has generated. The Government information campaign does not begin to tackle this problem. Trade unions, employers and workers in education all have a role to play in this area.

Trade unions

- Have a duty to their members to ensure no one is discriminated against at work because of AIDS hysteria. Fighting AIDS hysteria by providing information to members and giving full support to any members who experience discrimination in relation to AIDS is an integral part of a general fight against discrimination.

Employers

- Employers have a duty to be informed about AIDS.

- No one should be sacked from their job or harassed in any way because they are antibody positive.

- No employer should assume that because an employee is gay, he therefore has AIDS.

- No employee should ever be forced to take the HIV antibody test.

- Employers/organisations who have or who are developing Equal Opportunities Policies should ensure that the policy is designed to fight against discrimination which occurs as a result of AIDS hysteria.

- Conditions of service should be adapted to ensure that the right to compassionate leave is extended to lesbians and gay men. The need for compassionate leave to be extended to gay men has been highlighted by the advent of AIDS. It is important that employers are generous and sympathetic in their operation of compassionate leave to gay men (and obviously anyone else) who are caring for partners or close friends with AIDS.

Education

- Education authorities could devise an educational programme about AIDS for schools — an information programme which fights against AIDS hysteria and homophobia.

The NHS and health care

- AIDS is already a major public health problem and one which is likely to grow unless more public money is invested in research to fight the disease.

- The health service also needs more public money for the care and nursing of people with AIDS.

- In care and nursing for gay men who have AIDS the health service needs to be aware of issues which are particularly relevant to lesbians and gay men. For example, the health service needs to understand the importance of friendship and support networks in lesbian and gay communities. It is usually not appropriate for the health service to use narrow definitions of "next of kin" or family to decide who should and should not be included in the caring, nursing and decision making needed for gay men who are seriously ill as a result of AIDS.

Personal advice

- For anyone who is thinking of taking the HIV antibody test our advice is not to, without at least phoning the Terrence Higgins Trust first to discuss it.

- To anyone who has had the test our advice is not to tell your employer. It's none of their business. Even if the results of the test are negative, you may find that your employer wants you to take the test again at a later date.

EQUAL OPPORTUNITIES POLICIES

Employers and organisations should be developing comprehensive Equal Opportunities Policies to fight discrimination on the basis of sex, race, nationality, ethnic or national origin, religion, age, marital status, being people with disabilities, being lesbian or gay, being unemployed or having unrelated criminal convictions.

Although an EOP will differ with the type and structure of organisation, a basic framework can be followed which revolves around content, implementation and monitoring.

Content

- The content of an EOP should include a general policy statement which declares that the employer/organisation operates an equal opportunities policy. The statement should state which groups are covered by the policy. The terms "lesbians and gay men" should be used in the statement as opposed to the terms "sexual orientation" or "sexual preference".

- The general policy statement should be followed by a comprehensive Equal Opportunities Policy. The policy should detail specific strategy to be employed to fight each form of oppression identified in the policy statement. It is essential that throughout the policy it is taken into account that all oppression is inter-linked and interacting.

- An effective EOP gives protection to lesbians and gay men in an organisation by ensuring their right to be open at work and to be free from harassment. Harassment should be included in conditions of service as an act of misconduct to be dealt with under disciplinary and grievance procedures.

- Existing conditions of service should be comprehensively reviewed to ensure they apply equally to lesbians and gay men as to heterosexuals.

Bereavement and compassionate leave are examples of conditions of service which often discriminate against lesbians and gay men by the language used, for example, by referring to husbands and wives. Neutral terms which can be used instead are dependants and partners.

- The procedures used for recruitment and promotion often need to be changed when an EOP is put into operation. The use of interviews, personal records and references are all subject to the prejudice of individuals unless methods are devised to overcome such bias.

Implementation

- Making the policy work is crucial. All employees (including management) and users (service delivery and contract compliance) of an organisation should be made aware of the content of the policy and the implications it has for them.

- The policy should be widely advertised and a policy statement should accompany all job advertisements. Job advertisements should be placed in newspapers and magazines which are specifically aimed at the groups to which the policy is directed.

- Training is an important aspect of implementation. There are two main aspects of training required —

  1. Training to ensure that all employees are aware of the policy content and how to put it into operation. This should include the relevance of the policy to the day-to-day working environment.

  2. The provision of training courses aimed to counter the lack of opportunity many people have suffered in the educational system and in subsequent employment.

Monitoring and review

- An EOP must be constantly reviewed so that it can be adapted to every change in an organisation. Monitoring is needed to ensure that all groups in the community are represented in an organisation at all levels.

TRADE UNIONS

- Trade unions have a duty to their members to ensure that they represent the interests of all discriminated groups in the community.

- It is now official policy of the TUC, and thus all affiliated unions, to *actively* fight discrimination against lesbians and gay men.

- Each trade union should have a comprehensive EOP which details specific plans to fight discrimination on the basis of age, race, sex, religion, marital status, being lesbian or gay or people with disabilities. It is essential that when such policies are developed they are fully implemented and monitored at all levels in the union structure.

- It is important that trade unions develop and implement policies aimed to protect and inform members against AIDS hysteria and related discrimination. (See also recommendations under "AIDS".)

- Trade unions should be encouraging employers to develop comprehensive equal opportunities policies which include lesbians and gay men along the lines set out in chapter 5.

- All terms and conditions negotiated with employers should be scrutinised for heterosexual bias.

- Trade unions should support the right of any member to be openly lesbian or gay in their job. Any member who experiences discrimination by employers or co-workers because they are lesbian or gay should receive the full support of their union.

- In developing policy, trade unions must also recognise that many lesbians and gay men are discriminated against as a result of more than one form of oppression. Policies must take into account the effects of multiple oppression.

- Members need to be informed about lesbian and gay issues. Information should be disseminated at branch, regional and executive level.

- Self organised lesbian and gay trade union groups should be recognised and have the right to exist at all levels in the union structure. The right to self organisation should exist for all groups who suffer discrimination.

- Trade unions should be developing strategies to ensure that groups who are discriminated against are represented as officials at all levels in the union structure, including executive level.

■ Notes and References

CHAPTER 2: GAY WORKERS AND THE LAW

1. Many other examples and discussion of cases where lesbians and gay men have been dismissed because of their sexuality are given in *Gay Workers: Trade unions and the law*, by Chris Beer, Roland Jeffrey and Terry Munyard, published by NCCL, 1983. Two cases in this report which are particularly illustrative of both employers' and industrial tribunal panels' attitudes are *Burnham v. Trevor Page and Co Ltd* and *Bell v. Devon and Cornwall Police Authority*.

2. It is worth noting that employees who have been working for an employer for six months are entitled to ask for the reasons for their dismissal in writing from their employer. (The government is proposing to extend this period to two years.) These reasons must be supplied within 14 days of the request. An unreasonable refusal or a false reason will result in the employer being made to pay the sacked worker two weeks' pay. This provision can be used to pin down employers as to their reasons for sacking someone. Although many employers will doubtless disguise the true reason when it is anti-gay prejudice, the use of this right can prove helpful to the employee in showing irrational prejudice as the reason for dismissal.

3. Thus, while two stewards on a liner cannot lawfully have sex with each other or with crew members of another ship, either of them can have sex with a passenger. This anomaly is typical of the piecemeal and paranoid approach of British legislators when confronting the issue of gay sex.

4. The case of Brian, quoted from the evidence submitted by the Campaign for Homosexual Equality to the Select Committee on the Armed Forces Bill, illustrates this point.

> Brian joined the Royal Navy in 1979 aged 17. Although sensing he was gay at the time, he did not want to admit it to himself. In 1981 he was posted to HMS Apollo. In 1982, on a visit to London, he met another gay man for the first time.
>
> In November 1982, during shore leave, his prostrate was damaged when having sex. On return from leave he was very ill, but felt unable to explain the cause of the problem so it was diagnosed incorrectly. The illness persisted, so he explained its origin to the HMS Apollo Medical Officer who stressed the importance of proper medical treatment as soon as Brian reached HMS Nelson.
>
> His first two days at HMS Nelson were spent in a work party sweeping up leaves. On his second day there he was interviewed for three hours by a retired Lt Commander from the security services. Next he was sent to a psychiatrist, who offered to help him "overcome his disease" — if "help" was what he really wanted. Brian said he was gay and did not want to repress his homosexuality.
>
> Again he saw a medical officer, who, despite having Brian's papers, seemed not to believe he was ill, and gave no treatment. After four days at Nelson, Brian, who was now feeling extremely ill, was interviewed for about three hours by members of the Special Investigations Branch (SIB). Questioning centred on whether or not he had had sex with others in the Navy and if he knew any other gay people in the Navy. His possessions

were then searched and many removed, including his medicines. Interrogation then continued for another eight hours. During this time he was threatened with prosecution for having sex while under the age of consent.

His possessions and pills were returned to him two days later, but he received no proper treatment. In three weeks at Nelson he lost one and a half stones in weight.

He was discharged from the Navy on 5th January 1983; his discharge documents recorded that his character was "exemplary". The stress of the previous weeks now proved too much for Brian — he had a nervous breakdown and attempted suicide.

5. See, for example, *Gays and the law* by Paul Crane, published by Pluto Press.

6. *Ibid*, page 14.

7. Guidelines issued by the Director of Public Prosecutions have advised that where the two men involved are of similar age, for example one is 21 and the other 19, and no prostitution or no corruption is involved then no prosecution should take place.

8. GALOP Annual Report 1985, page 5.

9. A series of industrial tribunal cases has decided that an employer may be found to have dismissed a worker fairly on suspicion of an offence even though a criminal court finds the person not guilty. Dismissal is often regarded as fair simply because cases take so long to come up for a jury trial. Employers are not expected to have to keep someone on their books, at work or suspended on full pay pending a trial. This could apply to someone suspected of committing a gay offence, and subsequently found not guilty.

10. According to the *Disclosures of criminal convictions of those with access to children,* Joint review by the Home Office and DHSS. First report July 1985.

11. *Ibid.*

12. A case which challenged the statutory requirements for industrial tribunal lay members is that of *Habib v. Elkington and Co Ltd. (1981).* Mr Habib had unsuccessfully applied for a post as a personnel manager with Elkington and Co Ltd. He claimed that he had been unlawfully discriminated against on racial grounds. When the case came before an industrial tribunal Mr Habib complained that the tribunal panel lay members did not include a person who had experience of Asian life or was a person of Asian origin. For this reason he did not attend the hearing. The tribunal rejected his complaint and dismissed his claim. Mr Habib appealed to the Employment Appeal Tribunal (EAT). He claimed that the industrial tribunal should have had an Asian lay member because of a statement made by Lord Jacques during the passage of the Race Relation Bill (1976). Lord Jacques said that steps would be taken to appoint to the panel of lay members, people who, in addition to their knowledge of employment, had also special knowledge or experience of relations between persons of different groups in the employment field.

The EAT held that the statement made by Lord Jacques did not affect the legal composition of industrial tribunals. The EAT stated that the *only* statutory requirement for tribunals was that at each hearing there should be a "chairman" (*sic*) and two lay members. The lay members should be taken one each from a panel of persons representative of employers and one from a panel of persons representative of employees.

13. 'Lay members of the industrial tribunals', *Employment Gazette*, March/April 1986. pp116-117.

14. According to the *Disclosure of criminal convictions of those with access to children. Op. cit.*

CHAPTER 3: DAY-TO-DAY WORK

1. In the course of our research we sent out two press releases to the gay press which asked for gay men in manual occupations or areas of employment where it was difficult or impossible to come out to contact LAGER and be interviewed. Although these press releases were printed in most of the press aimed at gay men no one came forward within the time schedule we could allow for interviewing.

CHAPTER 4: AIDS

1. The Terrence Higgins Trust Publication, *AIDS and HTLV III: Medical briefing*, gives a detailed account of the research and findings so far on AIDS and HIV. Much of the information about AIDS and HIV in this chapter is taken from the pamphlet. The Terrence Higgins Trust is a registered charity set up to inform, advise and help on AIDS.

2. HTLV III stands for Human T-cell Lymphotrophic Virus type III. LAV stands for Lymphadenopathy Associated Virus. There has been controversy in the medical world as to whether the virus should be named HTLV III or LAV. To settle this controversy the term HIV is now being used as an alternative to both. Some of the quotations in this chapter refer to HTLV III because they were recorded prior to this decision. HIV is a retrovirus which means that it uses certain unusual enzymes to reproduce itself.

3. In special laboratory conditions the virus has been isolated from blood, semen, saliva, tears, breast milk and urine. There is no evidence, however, that anyone has ever been infected by the virus by tears or saliva. The research is still unclear about urine and breast milk. What is clear is the the virus dies almost immediately after leaving the blood stream. Therefore urine and breast milk are likely to be a risk only at the time of leaving the body, if at all.

4. Royal College of Nursing AIDS guidelines are available from:
   Royal College of Nursing
   Publications Department
   20 Cavendish Square
   London W1M OAB
   Price £3.75 (includes postage).

5. Lorraine Trenchard 'AIDS — Anything to do with us?' *GLC Women's Committee Bulletin.*

CHAPTER 5: EQUAL OPPORTUNITIES

1. Page 20, *Changing the world.* Published by the GLC.

2. Replies were received from the London Boroughs of — Brent, Bexley, Camden, Ealing, Islington, Haringey, Lambeth, Richmond, Southwark, Waltham Forest and Wandsworth. The London Borough of Havering acknowledged the letter but sent no information.

CHAPTER 6: TRADE UNIONS

1. In the course of our research we wrote to each of the 89 trade unions affiliated to the TUC. We asked them if they had motions passed at conference or policy statements which included lesbians and gay men. We also asked if the union had produced any information about lesbians and gay men or information about AIDS.
2. An equal opportunities official in the National Association of Probation Officers has informed LAGER that NAPO is aiming to be the first trade union in Britain to negotiate an equal opportunities agreement that includes "sexual orientation" with their employers at a national level.
3. Although NALGO has clearly been progressive in trying to implement its lesbian and gay policy, there is still work to be done amongst its own members. At the June 1986 annual NALGO conference a composite motion by the West Glamorgan Branch submitted by the South Wales District Council, and by the British Gas Operations Branch submitted by the West Midlands District Council stated:

> Conference instructs NEC to ensure that a re-appraisal is made of the use of union funds, publicity and promotion, at present being given to the movement for lesbian and gay rights, in relation to other campaigns currently being operated by NALGO on the basis that the rights of any NALGO member are protected by the quality of NALGO representation and leadership and the lesbian and gay members should not be treated as a special category.

233,000 voted for the motion and 381,000 voted against. Although the motion was defeated. it is a cause for concern that in a union often regarded as a "model" union for lesbian and gay policies nearly two-fifths of the conference members voted for the motion.

A clearly homophobic amendment (which was rejected before the above motion was voted upon) was submitted by the South Wales District Council...

> Delete everything after "Conference instructs the NEC" and insert:
> "to change the present aggressive campaigning style, on behalf of Gays and Lesbians, which is proving to be counter-productive in that it appears to be giving wider prominence and publicity to Gays and Lesbians and as a result is giving offence to a majority of NALGO grass root membership.
> Conference feels that the rights of all members are adequately covered and protected by service conditions committees and that Lesbian and Gay members should not be treated as a special category."

381,000 voted against accepting the amendment and 223,000 voted for it.
4. The sections *Race* and *Unions* in the *Further Reading List* give useful publications for information about race, employment and trade unions.

■ Appendix I
The questionnaire

Throughout this survey we .ave asked many questions relating to
employment/unemployment, which you may have had recent experience of.
You may, if you wish, fill in sections relating to previous
periods of employment/unemployment. If you are retired and are
commenting on previous periods when you were either working
or unemployed then please tick this box. ☐

1. Age: Are you   16-25   ☐ 100
                 26-35   ☐ 101
                 36-45   ☐ 102
                 46-55   ☐ 103
                 56-65   ☐ 104
                 66 or over ☐ 105

2. Are you   Black   ☐ 200
                 Asian   ☐ 201
                 A member of any
                 other ethnic minority   (Tick relevant boxes)
                 group   ☐ 202
                 Jewish   ☐ 203
                 Irish   ☐ 204
                 White   ☐ 205

3. Do you consider yourself to be:

                 Working class   ☐ 300
                 Middle class   ☐ 301
                 Upper class   ☐ 302
                 None of the above ☐ 303

4. Is your first language English:

                 Yes   ☐ 400
                 No   ☐ 401

5. What sort of household do you live in:

         With parents/guardian   ☐ 500
         With other lesbian/gay flatmates   ☐ 501
         Alone   ☐ 502
         With straight flatmates   ☐ 503
         Other (Please specify)...........☐ 504
         ....

6. How long have you lived in London:

         All your life   ☐ 600
         Less than five years   ☐ 601
         5-10 years   ☐ 602
         10 or more years   ☐ 603

7. If you have not always lived in London, was your being gay an
important reason for moving here:
                 Yes   ☐ 700
                 No   ☐ 701

8. Are you a person with disabilities:

                 Yes   ☐ 800
                 No   ☐ 801

9. Are you working: Yes   ☐ 900
                 No   ☐ 901

10. If unemployed, have you worked since you left school/further education:

Yes   ☐ 1000
No   ☐ 1001

11 Do you have an occupation/ trade: (Please specify)
....
....

12.Have you ever been sacked for being gay:

Yes   ☐ 1200
No   ☐ 1201

13. Do you know any other lesbians/gay men at work:

Yes   ☐ 1300
No   ☐ 1301

14. Could you take a gay friend into work:

Yes   ☐ 1400
No   ☐ 1401

15. Would you take people you work beside into gay places:

Yes   ☐ 1500
No   ☐ 1501

16. Do the people you work beside discuss their personal lives
in front of you:
Yes   ☐ 1600
No   ☐ 1601

17 Would you feel free to discuss your life, in relation to your
being gay, in front of the people you work beside:

Yes   ☐ 1700
No   ☐ 1701

18. Are you expected to take a special friend to any social gatherings
at work:
Yes   ☐ 1800
No   ☐ 1801

19. Would your work colleagues react favourably to your taking another
man to a social gathering:
Yes   ☐ 1900
No   ☐ 1901

20. Are any of the people who work beside you lesbian or gay:

None   ☐ 2000
Some   ☐ 2001
Most   ☐ 2002
All   ☐ 2003

21. Are there any of the people who work beside you who are particularly
supportive of your being gay:

None   ☐ 2100
Some   ☐ 2101
Most   ☐ 2102
All   ☐ 2103

22. The last time that you applied for a job, did you state that you are gay:

Yes   ☐ 2200
No   ☐ 2201

84

23. Would you like to be able to be open about being gay:
    A) At work   Yes   ☐ 2300
                    No   ☐ 2301
    B) On your application form
                    Yes   ☐ 2302
                    No   ☐ 2303
    C) In an interview
                    Yes   ☐ 2304
                    No   ☐ 2305

24. Are you obligied to present a certain image at work, by for example wearing a suit or uniform:
                    Yes   ☐ 2400
                    No   ☐ 2401

25. If the answer to question 24 was no, would you feel free to dress and act in the same way you would outside of work:
                    Yes   ☐ 2500
                    No   ☐ 2501

26. Has your being gay ever led to any sort of trouble at work:
                    No   ☐ 2600
                    Yes (Please specify)

....
....
....
....

27. If the answer to question 26 was yes, was it resolved by taking it to:
    A) A trade union   Yes   ☐ 2700
                         No   ☐ 2701
    B) Management   Yes   ☐ 2702
                         No   ☐ 2703

28. Has A.I.D.S. and the public reaction to it changed:
    A) The circumstances in which you work:
                    Yes   ☐ 2800
                    No   ☐ 2801
    B) Your inclination to come out as gay at work
                    Yes   ☐ 2802
                    No   ☐ 2803

If you answered yes to A or B please give details in the space below

29. Are you a member of a trade union/staff association:
                    Yes   ☐ 2900
                    No   ☐ 2901

30. Would you pursue a gay related grievance at work beyond an informal level:
                    Yes   ☐ 3000
                    No   ☐ 3001

31. Would you take the grievance up with an area trade union/ staff association representative:
                    Yes   ☐ 3100
                    No   ☐ 3101

32. Would you expect your local union or staff association representative to support you:

Yes	☐ 3200
No	☐ 3201

33. Do you feel that your boss(es) would support you:

Yes	☐ 3300
No	☐ 3301

34. If you were charged with an offence, which had no heterosexual equivalent, e.g. for having sex with someone over the age of sixteen, but under the age of twenty-one, do you think that your employer would use this against you:

Yes	☐ 3400
No	☐ 3401

35. In an instance as in question 34, do you think that your union would support you:

Yes	☐ 3500
No	☐ 3501

36. Is your employer an equal opportunity employer:

Yes	☐ 3600
No	☐ 3601
Don't know	☐ 3602

37. Is your employer at present negotiating an equal opportunities policy:

No	☐ 3700
Yes(please specify)	☐3701

....
....

38. If your answer to question 37 was yes, do they specifically mention lesbians & gays, or sexual orientation, either in their job advertisments or in any other literature that they produce:

Yes	☐ 3800
No	☐ 3801

39. Do you think that such policies are effective:

Yes	☐ 3900
No	☐ 3901

40. How well do you understand the rules and regulations you have to abide by at work (written or unwritten):

Fairly well	☐ 4000
Partly	☐ 4001
Not at all	☐ 4002

41. Do you know if your employment/conditions of employment includes any of the following:

A) Partner as nominated next of kin:

Yes	☐ 4100
No	☐ 4101
Don't know	☐ 4102

B) Compassionate leave in the event of a partners illness or death:

Yes	☐ 4103
No	☐ 4104
Don't know	☐ 4105

C) Gay partners to be given benefits similar to those of married employees (including childcare provision):

Yes	☐ 4106
No	☐ 4107
Don't know	☐ 4108

42. Do you feel that there is anything else that your employer could do:

             Yes   ☐ 4200
             No   ☐ 4201
             Don't know   ☐ 4202

Please specify...
....

43. At work do people presume that you don't have children:

             Yes   ☐ 4300
             No   ☐ 4301

44. Are there creche facilities where you work:

             Yes   ☐ 4400
             No   ☐ 4401

45. Do you feel that your work environment has improved as a result of the struggles led by lesbians and gay men:

             Yes   ☐ 4500
             No   ☐ 4501

Do you think that the GLC's stand on lesbian & gay rights has helped gay men in the workplace:

             Yes   ☐ 4600
             No   ☐ 4601

Please tick any of the relevant boxes below:
I would like to know more about LAGER's activities   ☐

I would like to be interviewed by LAGER   ☐

There is space overleaf to comment on any of the questions, or any of LAGER's activities.

N.B. The responses to some of the questions in the questionnaire have not been mentioned in the text. The results of these questions showed that the questionnaire was clearly inadequate to allow only for a Yes/No response. We could not analyse these questions in the absence of further explanation of the way in which each respondent interpreted them.

THE INTERVIEWEES

Below is a list of the gay men interviewed with a brief description of their work histories and personal characteristics. When the length of time in their present job is given, it is the time at the date of interview. None of the interviewees defined themselves as Jewish or as having disabilities.

Adam is a cycle courier for a dispatch firm. Prior to this, he had an MSC job painting murals. Before that, he had been unemployed for about three years after leaving college. He is white and defined himself as middle class.

Ainsley is a telephonist with a local authority. He has been there for six months. Before the council he was a shop assistant, a trainee hotel manager, and prior to this he worked for four and a half years with British Telecom. He is white, under 25 and defined himself as working class.

Alex is a university lecturer. Before this he taught in schools. He is white and defined himself as middle class.

Barry now works in the gay pub "The Two Brewers", because he was sacked from his previous job as a storekeeper with Smithfield Meters, for being gay. His jobs before that were in Scunthorpe and Doncaster. They included working in the motor trade and working for vending operators. He is white and defined himself as working class.

Ben did not wish his occupation to be disclosed. He is white and defined himself as middle class.

Bill has worked for the health service doing clerical work for the last two months. Previously he temped for two years. He is under 25 years of age, white and defined himself as working class.

Brian has been a primary school teacher for seven years. He has worked in several different schools and has been with his present school less than a year. Before training as a teacher he was a trainee manager in a hotel. He is white and defined himself as working class.

Gary works for a trade union support group. His previous jobs include working as an assistant in restaurants and cafes, and unfinished training as a chef (made redundant). He is Scottish, white and defined himself as working class.

Jim is unemployed. Prior to this he worked as a carpenter, a printer, office worker and salesperson. He is Afro-Caribbean. We do not have a definition of his class.

John is a chief technician in a university. He has been in his present job for about five years but with the university itself for about 11 years. Before the university he worked as a technician in a school for about four years, and as a clerk for two years. He is white and defined himself as working class.

Ken has been a librarian for the last six years. In this time he has worked for two local authorities. He is white and defined himself as middle class.

Kevin has been a residential social worker for approximately one year. Before social work he ran a youth club, and before that did other youth work in Ireland. He is white, Irish and defined himself as middle class.

Martin was a trainee manager with the GLC. Before the GLC he worked for the Terrence Higgins Trust on a paid basis for six to seven months. Prior to this he worked for a finance company. He is white, under 25 and did not use a definition of class.

Michael has been a punch operator with the DHSS for almost a year. Before, he was unemployed for one year nine months after leaving school. He is white, under 25 and defined himself as working class.

Steven is presently unemployed and has been for two months. His last job was with a retail store. Prior to this he worked as an insurance claims negotiator and a credit controller. He is white and did not define his class.

Sam has been an office worker for the last two years. Prior to this he worked for an escort agency and before this was unemployed. He is white, under 25 and defined himself as working class. (Did not have face-to-face interview. Quote in text was written and submitted to LAGER.)

Terry has been a charge nurse for the last two and a half years. Before that he was a staff nurse for two years and before that he was doing his three-year SRN training. Before nursing he worked as a porter, and a community worker. He is white and we do not have a definition of his class.

Winston has been a finance assistant for the last ten years. Before that he was an assistant accountant. He is Afro-Caribbean and defined himself as working class.

◼ Appendix II
Local authorities

Replies from London boroughs received by LAGER in response to a letter requesting information about Equal Opportunities included the following information —

Brent — EOP includes race, sex, colour, nationality or ethnic origins, age, marital status, sex, sexual orientation, disability or is disadvantaged by conditions or requirements which cannot be justifiable. A booklet explains their policies.

Bexley — Have policy statement which includes no discrimination on the grounds of colour, race, creed, nationality, ethnic or national origin, sex or marital status. The statement appears in all staff handbooks and is sent to all job applicants.

Camden — EOP includes sex, marital status, race, ethnic or national origin, religion or creed, disability, age, being lesbian or gay, unrelated criminal convictions. A booklet explains their policies. Also leaflets and a newsletter on equal opportunities.

Ealing — A policy statement commits the borough to the development of positive policies to promote equal opportunities in employment regardless of workers' sex, marital status, creed, colour, race or ethnic origins. At the time of going to press the inclusion of "sexual orientation" was being negotiated.

Haringey — Have EOP for which the policy statement is printed in the EOP chapter, page 50. A document explains their policies.

Islington — EOP includes race, colour, national or ethnic origin, sex, marital status, sexuality (being lesbian or gay), disability, class, age or religious belief. A document explains the policies.

Lambeth EOP includes race, colour, creed, ethnic or national origin, disabilities, age, sex, sexual orientation or marital status. A document explains their policies.

Richmond — EOP includes sex, sexual orientation, age, disability, marital status, creed/religion, colour, ethnic or national origin. An extensive report by the head of personnel services details a plan of action for implementation.

Southwark — EOP includes race, colour, ethnic and national origins, sex, marital status, domestic circumstances, sexual orientation, age, class, ethical beliefs, basic skills or trade union activity. A booklet explains their policies.

Waltham Forest — A statement of intent includes no discrimination on the grounds of race, colour, creed, ethnic or national origins, disabilities, age, sex, marital status or sexual orientation in any matters to do with employment. The statement is sent to all job applicants.

Wandsworth — EOP includes colour, race, nationality or ethnic or national origins, marital status, or sex.

Those boroughs which did not reply to the letter sent by LAGER were contacted by telephone. Of these boroughs, those which said they had actual policies (not just a policy statement) of no discrimination against lesbians and gay men or sexual orientation are Greenwich, Hackney, Hounslow and Lewisham.

Appendix III
AIDS: The trade union response

TABLE 1
AIDS: The trade union response

Trade union	Circular to branches/ safety reps etc.	Article in union journal	Leaflet or booklet	Other comments
Association of Cinematograph, Television and Allied Technicians	no	no	no	A recently formed "gay men and lesbians working party" may soon turn their attention to this issue
Association of Professional, Executive, Clerical and Computing Staff	no	no	no	Will be featured in the union journal during 1986 and possibly in a new health and safety section in the Apex reps' handbook to be issued during 1986
Association of University Teachers	yes	no	no	An AUT representative sits on the government's Advisory Committee on Dangerous Pathogens who draw up AIDS guidelines
Bakers, Food and Allied Workers Union	yes	yes	no	November 1985 issue of union journal
Broadcasting and Entertainment Trades Alliance	no	yes	no	November 1985 issue of union journal
Confederation of Health Service Employees	yes	no	yes	A 52-page detailed booklet on AIDS (price £2) has sold 10,000 copies and will be updated during 1986
Electrical, Electronic Telecommunication and Plumbing Union	yes	no	no	
Fire Brigades Union	yes	yes	no	Union journal, March 1985

TABLE 1 (cont)

Trade union	Circular to branches/ safety reps etc.	Article in union journal	Leaflet or booklet	Other comments
Furniture, Timber and Allied Trades Union	no	no	yes	Leaflet was specifically for funeral workers who may handle cases of AIDS
General, Municipal, Boilermakers and Allied Trades Union	no	no	yes	A detailed nine-page booklet produced in February 1985
Health Visitors Association	yes	no	no	Another circular on AIDS is due out soon
National and Local Government Officers' Association	yes	yes	yes	220,000 copies of Nalgo's leaflet on AIDS have been distributed. See *Nalgo News*, 6 December 1985
National Association of Schoolmasters/Union of Women Teachers	no	no	no	Will be producing something in the near future
National Association of Teachers in Further and Higher Education	no	yes	no	*Natfhe Journal*, December 1985
National Union of Journalists	no	yes	yes	Revised guidelines for members on reporting on AIDS are being prepared
National Union of Marine Aviation and Shipping Transport Officers	no	yes	no	April 1985 issue of Numast's *The Telegraph*
National Graphical Association (1982)	no	no	no	Has confidential contacts with the Terrence Higgins Trust should an NGA member approach the trust for advice

TABLE 1 (cont)

Trade union	Circular to branches/ safety reps etc.	Article in union journal	Leaflet or booklet	Other comments
National Union of Mineworkers	yes	no	no	TUC guidance on AIDS transmitted to areas. The recent strike has been the main reason for no article on AIDS appearing in union journal
National Union of Public Employees	yes	yes	yes	Very comprehensive material has been produced by Nupe; including a detailed study of the need for extra funding for AIDS
National Union of Railwaymen	yes	yes	no	The matter is being further pursued by the occupational health sub-committee of the Railway Industry Advisory Committee
National Union of Seamen	no	yes	no	*The Seaman*, March 1985
Society of Civil and Public Servants	yes	yes	no	Guidance issued to 3,600 safety reps
Transport and General Workers' Union	yes	yes	no	*TGWU Record*, October 1985; see text for resolution adopted on AIDS
Union of Communication Workers	yes	no	no	Three articles on AIDS have appeared in the union's branch officers' bulletin in February, March and May 1985
Union of Shop, Distributive and Allied Workers	yes	no	no	Circular was sent to members of the union involved in funeral furnishing

The table is reprinted with kind permission from the Journal "Labour Research" February 1986, Volume 75 Number 2. Published by the Labour Research Department, 78 Blackfriars Road, London SE1 8HF. Price £1.10.

■ Appendix IV
Further information

GROUPS (NATIONAL AND LONDON BASED)

Employment and Legal

Lesbian and Gay Employment Rights
(LAGER)
Room 203 Southbank House
Black Prince Road
London SE1 7SJ
01-587 1636 (Lesbians Only)
01-587 1643

Gay London Police Monitoring Group
(GALOP)
BM GALOP
London WC1 3XX
01-278 6215

Gay Legal Advice Service (GLAD)
BM GLAD
London WC1N 3XX
01-821 7672 (Mon-Fri 7-10pm)

National Council for Civil Liberties
(NCCL)
21 Tabard Street
London SE1
01-403 3888

Lesbian and Gay Trade Union Groups

CPSA Lesbian and Gay Group
271 Kensal Road
London W10
01-672 0316 (evenings only)

Gay Teachers Group
BM Gay Teacher
London WC1N 3XX

NALGO Met District Lesbian and Gay
Group
c/o 7 Pickwick Court
London SE9

Lesbians and Gays in BIFU
c/o Peter Freeman
2 Gwynfryn Road
Pontardulais
Swansea
SA4 1LG
0792 884153 (evenings and weekends)

Lesbians and gays in NAPO
3/4 Chiwalty Road
Battersea
London SW11 1AT

ACTT Lesbian and Gay Working Party
c/o D. Abbott
2 Soho Square
London
W1V 6DD

Gay Welfare Workers Group
c/o 100c Knightshill
West Norwood
London SE27

Teachers in Higher & Further Education
    Gay Group
c/o 5 Caledonian Road
London N1

NUJ Lesbian and Gay Group
BM NUJ LGG
London WC1N 3XX

Sexuality in Social Work
Peter 01-732 1369
Joset 01-471 0996

NUS Lesbian and Gay Group (students)
461 Holloway Road
London N7

Labour Movement

Labour Campaign for Lesbian and
    Gay Rights (LCLGR)
c/o T. Gleny
119 Riverdale Road
London N5 2SU

AIDS

Terrence Higgins Trust (THT)
BM AIDS
London WC1N 3XX
Helpline 01-833 2971
(7-10 every day)

Body Positive
Help and advice for people who are
    anti-body positive
BM AIDS
London WC1N 3XX

People with Disabilities

Gay Men's Disabled Group
c/o Gay's the Word Bookshop
London WC1N 1AB

Brothers and Sisters Group
For people who are deaf and hard
    of hearing
BM B&S
London WC1N 3XX

Gemma
For lesbians with disabilities
BM Box 5700
London WC1N 3XX

Young People

London Gay Teenage Group (LGTV)
01-272 5741 (Wed 7-10pm, Sun 3-5pm)

Lesbian and Gay Youth Movement
(LGYM)
BM GYM
London WC1N 3XX

South London Young Gay People
c/o Hearsay
17 Brownhill Road
Catford
London SE6
01-697 2152 (Tues 7-10pm)

Black and Ethnic Minority Groups

Lesbian and Gay Black Group (LGBC)
BM Box 4390
London WC1N 3XX

Black Lesbian and Gay Centre (BLGC)
Annex "B"
Tottenham Town Hall
High Road
London N15
01-701 4073 (women only)
01-800 1359

Women's Projects

A list of the London area Women's Centres and groups can be obtained from:

A Woman's Place
Hungerford House
Victoria Embankment
London WC2
01-836 6081

Media

Campaign for Press and Broadcasting
   Freedom (CPBF)
9 Poland Street
London W1V 3DG

Capital Gay
38 Mount Pleasant
East Block
2nd Floor
London WC1

General

Campaign for Homosexual Equality
(CHE)
c/o 274 Upper Street
London N1 2UA
01-359 3973

Lesbian and Gay Switchboard
(Information Service)
24 hour telephone service
01-837 7324

London Friend
(Befriending Organisation)
33a Seven Sisters Road
London N7 6AR
01-359 7371

London Lesbian and Gay Centre
67-69 Cowcross Street
London EC1
01-608 1471

Gay's the Word Bookshop
66 Marchmont Street
London WC1N 1AB
01-278 7654

There are many lesbian and gay groups not listed here. For more information, contact Lesbian and Gay Switchboard (01-837 7324).

Glossary of words used in this report

HETEROSEXISM — Discrimination against lesbians and gay men by hetero-sexuals on an individual and institutional level. The use of the word in this report follows the definition put forward in *Challenging heterosexism in the workplace* by the GLC Equal Opportunities Group.

> Heterosexism is a set of assumptions and practices which serve to promote heterosexuality (relationships between women and men). Heterosexism as a system states that the only valid "normal" and "natural" forms of relationship are heterosexual ones. Heterosexism sets out to penalise those who do not conform to heterosexuality and reward those that do. Thus heterosexuality is also an institutionalised form of discrimination, since all institutions in our society discriminate against those who are not heterosexual, i.e. lesbians and gay men.

HOMOPHOBIA literally means "fear of the same". Used in this report to describe fear of loving and fear of relationships with members of the same sex. Fear resulting in hatred and contempt for lesbians and gay men.

LESBIAN — A woman who loves other women emotionally and sexually.

GAY was used in the past, and sometimes still is, to describe both women and men who relate to the same sex. Gay is used in this report to describe only men who love other men emotionally and sexually. Using gay to refer to women and men fails to distinguish lesbians and gay men as different groups which suffer discrimination.

SEXISM — The oppression of women by men at both the personal and institutional level.

RACISM — The systematic oppression of people on account of their colour or racial origin. It is based on racial prejudice, the willingness to discriminate and the power to deny someone justice and equality because of their racial origin. Deep-rooted racial prejudice and racism exist in all spheres of social, political and cultural life in Britain as a result of slavery, colonialism, imperialism and capitalism. It exists at an individual and institutional level.

PEOPLE WITH DISABILITIES —

> …are not always an easily identifiable group. Many people have invisible disabilities like diabetes, epilepsy or heart disease.
> They are not a static, unchanging group either. Some people born with disabilities partially or even totally lose them. Others may become disabled — for example in a car crash or while playing a hazardous sport, or because of carelessly prescribed drugs.
> *More Than Ramps.* Published by NALGO.

People with disabilities experience discrimination in...

...every area of life: personal relationships, education, employment, housing, services, access to public buildings, leisure and recreational facilities (and reproductive rights).

Having a disability, even a severe one, by itself does not mean a person cannot take part in the daily activities the rest of us take for granted, although some people with disabilities need assistance to do so. It is our *attitudes* and the *obstacles* we create for people with disabilities that turn a *disability* into a *handicap* and seriously limit their ability to participate in the community.

Disability Shouldn't be a Handicap
Published by the GLC Disability Resource Team

COMING OUT — A process which involves individuals acknowledging to themselves and to others that they are lesbian or gay.

OUT/BEING OUT — Refers to lesbians and gay men who are open with others about their sexuality.

■ Further Reading

The following list of publications is of books, pamphlets and leaflets which contain information about rights at work, measures to fight discrimination in employment or unemployment, or accounts of discrimination.

LESBIAN AND GAY

Changing the World: A charter for gay and lesbian rights, produced by the GLC.

Danger Heterosexism at Work. Published by the Industry and Employment Branch of the GLC. Available free from the London Strategic Policy Unit, Publications Department, Middlesex House, 20 Vauxhall Bridge Rd., London SW1V 2SB.

Gays and the Law by Paul Crane. Published by Pluto Press.

Gay Workers: Trade unions and the Law by Chris Beer *et al*. Published by the National Council for Civil Liberties.

What about the Gay Workers? Published by the Campaign for Homosexual Equality.

LESBIANS

All in a Day's Work edited by Nina Taylor. Published by Lesbian Employment Rights.

Tackling Heterosexism. Published by the GLC Women's Committee. Available free from the Women's Equality Group, Middlesex House, 20 Vauxhall Bridge Rd., London SW1V 2SB.

YOUNG LESBIANS AND GAYS

Something to Tell You by Lorraine Trenchard and Hugh Warren. Published by the London Gay Teenage Group (LGTG).

Young Lesbians by Lorraine Trenchard. Published by LGTG.

PEOPLE WITH DISABILITIES

To our knowledge there are no publications which focus on gay men with disabilities. Some useful publications regarding people with disabilities in relation to unemployment and employment are as follows:

Code of Good Practice on the Employment of Disabled People. Published by the Manpower Services Commission (MSC). Leaflets are also available from the MSC.

Disability Shouldn't be a Handicap. Published by the GLC Disability Resource Team.

Employers' Guide to Disability. Published by the Royal Association for Disability and Rehabilitation (RADAR).

Into Work: A guide for Disabled People. Published by RADAR.

The Adoption of Jobs and the Employment of the Disabled. Published by the International Labour Office. Only available from The International Labour Office, Publications Branch CH-1211 Geneva 22, Switzerland.

RACE

To our knowledge no publications exist which focus on Black gay men in the UK. An American publication *In the Life — Black Gay Anthology* edited by Joseph Beam will shortly be available in Britain. A few of many useful publications which focus on Black people generally in relation to un/ employment are as follows:

Black workers, trade unions and the law: a negotiator's guide. Labour Research Department.

CRE Code of Practice — for the elimination of racial discrimination and the promotion of equal opportunity in employment. Published by the Commission for Racial Equality.

Employment, unemployment and Black people by Anne Newham. Published by the Runnymede Research Project.

Racial Discrimination — Your Rights to Equal Opportunity by Michael Malone. Published by Ross Anderson.

UNIONS

NALGO Lesbian and Gay Rights Organising Pack. Available free from NALGO, 1 Mabledon Place, London WC1H 9AJ.

Black Workers and Trade Unions information and organising pack by the Greater London Trade Union Resource Unit. Produced by the South East Region Trade Union Congress.

Racism Within Trade Unions: Challenging racism at work and in the trade unions. Produced by the Greater London Council's Anti-Racist Trade Union Working Group

TUC guide on the employment of disabled people. Produced by the TUC.

Getting Organised by Allan Campbell and John McIlroy. Published by Pan.

GENERAL EMPLOYMENT RIGHTS

Rights at Work by Jeremy McMullen. Published by Pluto Press.

AIDS

AIDS: a guide to survival by Peter Tatchell. Published by GMP.

Panic: the story of AIDS by Robin McKie. Published by Thorsons.

AIDS: the new puritanism by Dennis Altman. Published by Pluto Press.